HILDEGARD OF BINGEN

WOMEN

Composers

The short, readable books in the Women Composers series
introduce significant women composers to students and
general readers and provide a convenient reference for
performers and scholars.

Series books treat the broadest range of women
composers, combining concise biographical information
with a comprehensive survey of works.

A list of books in the series appears at the end of this book.

Hildegard
of Bingen

Honey Meconi

**UNIVERSITY OF
ILLINOIS PRESS**
Urbana, Chicago, and Springfield

1 2 3 4 5 C P 5 4 3 2 1

⊗ This book is printed on acid-
free paper.

Publication of this book is supported by the Margarita
M. Hanson Endowment of the American Musicological
Society, funded in part by the National Endowment for the
Humanities and the Andrew W. Mellon Foundation.

Library of Congress Cataloging-in-Publication Data
Names: Meconi, Honey, author.
Title: Hildegard of Bingen / Honey Meconi.
Description: Urbana : University of Illinois Press, [2018]
| Series: Women composers | Includes bibliographical
references and index.
Identifiers: LCCN 2017059137| ISBN 9780252033155
(hardcover : alk. paper) | ISBN 9780252083679 (pbk. : alk.
paper)
Subjects: LCSH: Hildegard, Saint, 1098–1179. | Women
composers—Germany—Biography. | Composers—
Germany—Biography.
Classification: LCC ML410.H618 M43 2018 | DDC 782.25092
[B]—dc23
LC record available at https://lccn.loc.gov/2017059137

E-book ISBN 978-0-252-05072-5

In loving memory of my mother

Mary Evelyn Lewis Meconi

November 18, 1924–January 3, 2010

CONTENTS

ILLUSTRATIONS

ACKNOWLEDGMENTS

Because I have been performing Hildegard's music since 1982, it is impossible to thank everyone who has been part of the long journey toward this book. But some names must still be singled out. Of the many who have helped along the way, I am first of all deeply grateful to Laurie Matheson for approaching me about this book and for her patience and encouragement as it progressed. I extend my thanks as well to Julie Laut, also of the University of Illinois Press, for her help with production. Thanks must also go to Dr. Monica Maria Angeli of the Biblioteca Statale di Lucca; Dr. David Burn, Dr. Bart Demuyt, and Dr. Ann Kelders of the Alamire Foundation; Dr. Martin Mayer of the Hochschul- und Landesbibliothek RheinMain; Sister Philippa Rath, OSB, of the Abtei St. Hildegard; Dr. Jürgen Ritter of the Bayerische Staatsbibliothek; Dr. Matthias Schmandt of the Museum am Strom, Bingen; and Dr. Günther Stanzl for their invaluable assistance with illustrations. I am indebted as well to the College of Arts, Sciences, and Engineering at the University of Rochester for their generous subvention toward publication costs, and I am deeply appreciative for the subvention provided by the Margarita M. Hanson Endowment of the American Musicological Society, funded in part by the National Endowment for the Humanities and the Andrew W. Mellon Foundation.

Any volume dealing with Hildegard's music owes a great deal to those who have also written about or performed her glorious works. Especially important in that category are the following, many of whom I have the privilege to know personally: Peter Dronke, Barbara Newman, Marianne Richert Pfau, Stefan Morent, Barbara Stühlmeyer, Margot Fassler, Jennifer Bain, Christopher Page, and Stevie Wishart. Marianne Richert Pfau must be thanked again, along with an anonymous reader, for numerous helpful suggestions when I first submitted the manuscript; I am grateful for their advice. I would also like to acknowledge Michael Embach, Sarah Higley, and Herta Weller-Chutsch, as well as my wonderful husband and perfect son, for their contributions in manifold ways. In addition, I am forever indebted to Janet Rich and her family for first taking me to Villers Abbey on August 15, 1981, when neither they nor I could have dreamed where that visit would lead.

Finally, there are many ways for a woman to make a difference in the world. One example is that of Hildegard. Another is that of my mother, my beloved role model, to whose memory this book is dedicated.

HILDEGARD OF BINGEN

1 | Before Rupertsberg

Composer. Poet. Performer. Dramatist. Visionary. Prophet. Theologian. Exegete. Cosmologist. Spiritual leader. Preacher. Exorcist. Philosopher. Founder. Correspondent. Political advisor. Monastic troubleshooter. Hagiographer. Naturalist. Medical writer. Linguist. Noblewoman. Nun. *Magistra*. Teacher. Healer. Autobiographer. All of these roles describe Hildegard of Bingen.

Many know Hildegard today foremost or even exclusively as a composer, and her achievements in this area are indeed noteworthy: the most prolific composer of plainchant; one of the earliest—male or female—that we know by name; creator of the first musical "morality play" (and the only one for whom we have a named composer); and composer of seventy-seven songs, all but one set to her own idiosyncratic poetry in a distinctive and glorious musical style. But just as her music, all plainchant, distinguishes her from the many other feisty and creative spiritual women of the twelfth century, so, too, do her nonmusical accomplishments separate her from virtually all other major composers (whether of the Middle Ages or later times), few of whom are known for anything but composition, and almost none of whom are of equal significance in another field.[1] Yet during her lifetime and until very recently it was not Hildegard's music that led to her fame; rather, it was her spirituality. Indeed, Hildegard's was a holistic life, and her music can only be understood as one facet of a creativity that mirrored and was generated by her religious beliefs.

Simply put, Hildegard was a visionary. She literally "saw things" that she claimed were revealed to her by God, and in her early forties—she lived to be eighty-one—she began writing these things down. Over a productive span of almost forty years she generated three major theological works: *Scivias* (Know the Ways), *Liber vite meritorum* (Book of Life's Merits), and *Liber divinorum operum* (Book of Divine Works); two works of hagiography (lives of St. Rupert and St. Disibod); several smaller theological writings (a commentary on the Benedictine Rule, a commentary on the Athanasian Creed, a series of homilies on the Gospels, and a set of answers to thirty-eight questions sent to her by Cistercian monks); an extensive correspondence of almost four hundred letters and replies, the list of whose recipients reads like a who's who of twelfth-century Europe; a volume of natural history (*Physica*); the medical treatise *Cause et cure* (Causes and Cures); an invented language (*Lingua ignota*, Unknown Language) and accompanying alphabet (*Litterae ignotae*, Unknown Letters); perhaps works of art (sketches for the illustrations that accompany one manuscript of *Scivias*); an exorcism ritual; an autobiography; and, of course, her musical play, *Ordo virtutum* (usually translated as "The Play of the Virtues"), and her songs, commonly known as the *Symphonia armonie celestium revelationum* (Symphony of the Harmony of the Celestial Revelations).[2] Almost all of these works are included in a massive manuscript begun toward the end of her life known as the Riesencodex (Giant Codex), and all result from a holistic concept of creation.

We know of Hildegard's works through the Riesencodex and other manuscripts, and we also—unusually for the Middle Ages—have a great deal of information about her life. Biographical material is sprinkled throughout her correspondence and appears as well in the prefaces to some of her works. And since Hildegard achieved a considerable amount of fame during her lifetime, others wrote about her both while she was still alive and for some time after her death. Close to the end of her life, her secretary Gottfried of Disibodenberg began a *vita*, the standard biographical work for saints and those perceived as saintly. Finished after his (and Hildegard's) death by the monk Theoderic of Echternach, the *Vita Sanctae Hildegardis* (hereafter *Vita*) included autobiographical portions by Hildegard herself.[3] A second vita was begun but never finished by Hildegard's last secretary, Guibert of Gembloux (sometimes referred to as Wibert), who also left a set of revisions for the Gottfried/Theoderic *Vita*, as well as a series of letters to various correspondents that contain additional material on Hildegard. Eight readings generated after her death and used on her feast day provide another source of information, as does the early thirteenth-century *Acta inquisitionis de virtutibus et miraculis S. Hildegardis* (Acts of the Inquiry into the Virtues and Miracles of Hildegard), a document drawn up in connection with Hildegard's canonization proceedings.

In contrast to almost all other medieval composers, then, we have a vast amount of information about Hildegard's life. Unfortunately, large gaps still remain, few dates are firm, and many contradictions mar the material that survives. Just how accurate all these sources are is another very big question. As a result, the story of her life as we know it today is both intensely frustrating (how much is true?) and extraordinarily thrilling.

Beginnings

Hildegard was the tenth child of noble parents, Mechtild and Hildebert of Bermersheim near Alzey in the diocese of Mainz. Although various later twelfth-century documents offer a birth year of 1100, perhaps chosen for its symbolism, all three of Hildegard's major theological writings, which she is careful to date, point to an earlier birth year. In the preface to her first book, *Scivias*, Hildegard says that she was in her forty-third year in 1141, precisely stating her age as forty-two years and seven months. This could generate a birth date anywhere between June 1098 and May 1099. In the preface to *Liber vite meritorum*, however, she says both that she was sixty in 1158 and that it was the sixty-first year of her life, while in the preface to *Liber divinorum operum* she gives the year as 1163 and says that she is sixty-five. Both thus fix her birth date firmly in 1098. Finally, the *Vita* indicates that when Hildegard passed away on September 17, 1179, she was in the "82nd year of her life" and therefore eighty-one years old.[4] Her birthday was thus somewhere between June and mid-September of 1098.

Hildegard began having visions at an early age—the *Vita* puts these as far back as when she first learned to talk—and spoke of them artlessly until her fifteenth year, only gradually realizing that others did not see as she did.[5] Once she became aware of how different she was, she mostly kept things to herself until she was more than forty years old,[6] even though the visions continued. Only one of her earliest visions is known: according to the canonization report, the five-year-old Hildegard was able to tell the color and markings of an unborn calf.[7] In terms of her visions, Hildegard insisted throughout her life that she was a "poor little creature" and a "weak woman" whom God had chosen as a vessel for his message; it was never Hildegard speaking, she claimed, but rather the Holy Spirit acting through her.[8]

The vision of the unborn calf supposedly prompted her parents to consider what to do with their unusual daughter. In addition to seeing visions, Hildegard was a sickly child who would ultimately endure poor health for extended periods in her adult life, typically at moments of great stress. These two factors boded ill for the marriage market, and some have speculated that her parents had run out of money for a dowry for their last child. In any event, ultimately she was "offered to God." Guibert of Gembloux describes this act as a tithe on her parents' part,[9] but this seems unlikely given that three of her siblings were already dedicated to the Church. Moreover, the Church frequently served as a refuge for the frail offspring of noble families in the Middle Ages.

Like so much of Hildegard's early life, exactly when this "offering" occurred and what it consisted of is open to interpretation. Although the *Vita* says it took place in her eighth year (1105/1106), it was not until 1112—specifically on November 1, the Feast of All Saints—that Hildegard made a formal pact with the Church. She did not do this alone, but rather in the company of two other women, one of whom was to be her teacher and mentor for the next twenty-four years.

This woman was Jutta of Sponheim, a pious young woman a mere six years older than Hildegard. Member of a noble family somewhat more distinguished than Hildegard's, Jutta fell seriously ill at the age of twelve. Upon recovery she set about fulfilling a vow to pursue a holy life. Acting first as a disciple to a holy widow named Uda of Göllheim, she next planned a pilgrimage, but her brother dissuaded her from pursuing this idea. Instead, she opted for something much more dramatic: enclosure within the Benedictine monastery of Disibodenberg. And she took Hildegard with her.

Enclosure

Exactly when Hildegard met Jutta is unknown. One theory is that she came to Jutta in her eighth year, the time the *Vita* says Hildegard was offered to God, and that Hildegard lived at Sponheim with Jutta as the latter's own disciple. If so, this life was ultimately insufficient for either Hildegard or Jutta, and a more drastic step was taken. Hildegard, Jutta, and Jutta's niece (acting as their servant, and also named Jutta) chose Disibodenberg as their future home.

Disibodenberg—surviving today only in ruins, as seen in figure 1—was a new Benedictine community, founded on the site of an earlier dwelling whose Augustinian canons had been displaced in favor of the monks. Construction of the new monastery began on June 30, 1108,[10] with monks from the Mainz abbey of St. Jacob living at the site from at least the previous year. The building campaign

Figure 1. Disibodenberg ("Rudera coenobii Disibodenbergensis") from Georg Christian Joannis, *Tabularum litterarumque veterum usque hoc nondum editarum Spicilegium* (Frankfurt am Main: J. M. a Sande, 1724), 87.

included an impressively large church whose first altar was dedicated in 1130 and whose main altar was finally dedicated only in 1143. Most of Hildegard's life at Disibodenberg—where she would dwell longer than anywhere else—was thus lived to the accompaniment of the noise of construction. The monastery proper was restricted to a relatively contained territory at the top of a steep hill, though its property ownership—a major source of income—eventually spread over a wide area. At some point Jutta's own family gave property to the monastery as well. The monastery's site accords with the older Benedictine preference to build on mountaintops ("contemplative ascent to God") versus the Cistercian practice of gravitation to "isolated valleys, symbolizing humility."[11]

In the early twelfth century, double monasteries—a community of monks joined to a community of nuns—existed, but Disibodenberg did not begin as one of those. Jutta's relationship to the community was rather that of holy woman living within the monastery's walls and thus providing luster and the flavor of greater than usual sanctity to the community; the presence of an anchoress at a male monastery was not uncommon in the Mainz diocese. Jutta also chose the most extreme mode of living, that of strict enclosure, which permitted a single opening through which food could be passed and human waste removed. Thus on November 1, 1112, following a formal ceremony, Hildegard and the two Juttas were literally walled into their living space, with the understanding that they would leave that humble dwelling only upon their death. Hildegard's monastic profession, to Bishop Otto of Bamberg (later St. Otto), was made at some unspecified time, possibly the same day.[12]

Guibert describes the situation thus: "And so with psalms and spiritual canticles the three of them were enclosed in the name of the most high Trinity. After the assembly had withdrawn, there they were left in the hand of the Lord. Except for a rather small window through which visitors could speak at certain hours and necessary provisions be passed across, all access was blocked off, not with wood but with stones solidly cemented in."[13]

Further discussion of Jutta's enclosure by Guibert indicates that "in this way, she so provided herself with a haven of seclusion that she would not hinder the monks either by her own presence or by any of the visitors who approached her, or herself be hindered by anyone. On the other hand, far from the clamour of the crowd, she had free access by day and by night to the offices of the monks at their psalmody nearby."[14]

Enclosure provided security from physical harm—an eternal danger for women—but that was at most only a subliminal reason for undertaking such a drastic step. The primary impetus was for the better practice of spiritual piety. As Guibert says, "They earnestly inclined themselves to God with prayers and holy meditations, checking the urges of the flesh with constant fasts and vigils."[15] Jutta specifically matched the stereotype of the medieval holy woman and anchoress in virtually every respect. She wore "the cheapest and meanest of clothing" and both a hair shirt and an iron chain, normally right next to her body in order to maximize discomfort.[16] She went barefoot in the winter. She not only went through the psalter daily—and sometimes twice or three times per day—but did this standing or crouching, occasionally prostrating herself after every verse. She ate little, "contenting herself with the left-overs from the common table, though it be but a pauper's table,"[17] and abstained from meat for eight years.

In tandem with her fleshly mortification, Jutta interacted in saintly ways with others. People flocked to her; she offered counsel and prayer, and healed the sick with the laying on of her hands. Her fame spread widely; some came to see her, while those not living nearby wrote to ask for her prayers and advocacy. She was tart in her responses when necessary: "She was not one to prop up anyone's elbow with the cushions of flattery. For those who came to see her, she mixed the wine of stringent correction with the oil of sweet and humble counsel."[18] She received divine revelations, and she struck one unspiritual brother dumb and then restored him to health through her prayers.

Jutta also proved a magnet for other young women wishing to follow a holy life. According to Guibert, parents asked Jutta to take their daughters, offering as support gifts to the monastery of vineyards, property, and estates.[19] Jutta referred the matter to her superiors, who agreed with the requests. Thus, "When the entrance to her tomb was opened up, she [Jutta] brought inside with her the girls who were to be nurtured under the guidance of her disciplined guardianship. It was on this occasion that what was formerly a sepulchre became a kind of monastery, but in such a way that she did not give up the enclosure of the sepulchre, even as she obtained the concourse of a monastery."[20] No date is given for this massive change in Jutta's and Hildegard's lives.

Just what Hildegard learned from Jutta is difficult to determine. Benedictines revered learning, and Hildegard's prose writings show (though without naming sources) that she was intimately acquainted with an extremely wide range of both older and contemporary writing, and not merely the expected Bible and works by the Church Fathers. But how she acquired her knowledge is unclear. The Chronicles of Disibodenberg tell us that Jutta "strove to imbue [Hildegard and others] with holy virtues,"[21] a vague and unhelpful statement. Jutta is described as reading, but silently, and thus not in a way that might benefit Hildegard.[22] Hildegard's education gets but passing mention in the *Vita*, where an autobiographical passage frankly calls Jutta *indocta* (unschooled).[23] The *Vita* also says that "Jutta carefully fitted her for a garment of humility and innocence, and, instructing her in the songs of David, showed her how to play on the ten-string psaltery."[24] This last reference may be to the Ten Commandments (following Augustine's commentary on Psalm 150) rather than a real instrument.[25] The songs of David, on the other hand, are the psalms, which were normally sung rather than spoken in the Middle Ages. Somehow, though, Hildegard achieved familiarity with an enormous amount of literature beyond these biblical items. Yet with unflagging consistency she described herself as unlearned. This, of course, was the only possible strategy for her, as a woman, to be believed when she later made her pronouncements: God, not the unlearned Hildegard, was responsible for what she was saying.

Magistra

Just over twenty-four years after Jutta and Hildegard had been enclosed at Disibodenberg, Jutta passed away at the age of forty-four. The day of her death was announced to her in a vision; when the time approached, she asked the ten women of her community to put her on a "hair-mat in a place convenient for the arrival of the brothers."[26] As the monks prayed litanies over her, she died on December 22, 1136.

After Jutta's death, Hildegard and two other women took care of arranging the body, discovering when they undressed her that "a chain which she had worn on her flesh had made three furrows right around her body,"[27] although the body itself shone with a miraculous whiteness. Jutta's funeral attracted clerical and secular leaders as well as a huge crowd of women and men from all walks, classes, and ages of life. Buried first in the monastery's chapter house, her body was later interred immediately before the altar in the Marian chapel.[28]

Five days after Jutta's death, the archbishop of Mainz ordained a new abbot of Disibodenberg: Cuno, whose name also appears as Cuono and Kuno. About the same time, the ten disciples Jutta left unanimously chose Hildegard, her first follower, as their new leader. Thus, the heads of both the women's and the men's communities at Disibodenberg assumed their new roles at almost exactly the same time, but their relationship was decidedly not one of equals. Hildegard, for example, did not have the title "abbess"; she was referred to instead only as *magistra* (variously translated as chief, master, director, advisor, guardian, etc.).

Some years after Jutta's death, Hildegard asked for a vita of Jutta to be written. This vita refers to the late Otto of Bamberg (d. June 30, 1139; canonized 1189), the same person who heard Hildegard's monastic vows, so it obviously postdates that event. The descriptions of Jutta's life and actions in the vita follow the stereotypical saintly model, but the account also describes in detail a vision that Hildegard had concerning how Jutta's soul fared after her death; Hildegard is identified as Jutta's "first and most intimate disciple."[29] A possible author of the vita was the monk Volmar (also known as Fomar or Fulmar), Hildegard's confessor, advisor, and friend until his death in 1173.

If Hildegard had continued as Jutta had lived, we would almost certainly not care or even know about her today; her life would have followed the pattern of numerous holy women whose existence was largely private or entirely anonymous. But in 1141 everything changed. Hildegard—at the precise age of forty-two years and seven months, more than halfway through her life—had a vision unlike any other she had ever experienced: "Heaven was opened and a fiery light of exceeding brilliance came and permeated my whole heart and my whole brain."[30] Two key components distinguished this life-changing event. First, knowledge and understanding of all types came to her instantly in divine revelation: "And immediately I knew the meaning of the exposition of the Scriptures, namely the Psalter, the Gospel and the other catholic volumes of both the Old and the New Testaments, though I did not have the interpretation of the words of their texts or the division of the syllables or the knowledge of cases or tenses."[31] Second, God commanded her to make known what was revealed: "O fragile human, ashes of ashes, and filth of filth! Say and write what you see and hear!"[32] And thus began a life of creative production unparalleled among medieval women and men.

The account of this miraculous vision appeared first in the preface to Hildegard's theological treatise *Scivias*, the immediate result of God's command. The preface lays out the underlying themes that inform all of Hildegard's writings: it is God's word that is transmitted, not hers; she is a lowly creature, humble, fearful, and timid, whom God has chosen as his vessel; she is unlearned. To emphasize the reason that Hildegard is writing, the preface returns again and again to his command: "Thus therefore, O human, speak these things that you see and hear"; "Speak therefore of these wonders, and, being so taught, write them and speak"; "O human, who receives these things meant to manifest what is hidden not in the disquiet of deception but in the purity of simplicity, write, therefore, the things you see and hear"; and the very last words of the preface: "And again I heard a voice from Heaven saying to me, 'Cry out therefore, and write thus!'"[33]

Despite the fivefold command to get to work, Hildegard responded as she did throughout her life when confronted with a difficult or stressful situation: she fell ill. The *Scivias* preface tells us that two people—unnamed in the book—finally compelled her to write. Each was to play a key role in later years. One was her favorite nun, the noblewoman Richardis von Stade. The other was the monk who became her faithful amanuensis for the rest of his life, Volmar of Disibodenberg; figure 2 shows Volmar looking on as Hildegard is inspired by the Holy Spirit. With help from others, then, she started her first visionary treatise. But on her own she took a dramatic step that, in retrospect, was entirely typical of her: she wrote a letter to Bernard of Clairvaux.

Bernard of Clairvaux (1090–1153)—who became St. Bernard barely two decades after his death—was one of the most famous ecclesiastics of his time. He was a member of the Cistercians, a monastic order founded in 1098 that emphasized a more ascetic rule than did the much older Benedictines. Bernard was abbot and founder of the Clairvaux monastery and was noted for his guidance to popes and other churchmen as well as for his many theological writings; he also was a vigorous promoter of the disastrous Second Crusade, begun in 1147.

Hildegard's letter to Bernard (Letter 1), from 1147,[34] is a personal but straightforward request for his guidance, laying out her dilemma: did God intend for her to write what she had seen? Her request is timidly put, in strong contrast to virtually all the rest of her correspondence. It is also an odd request in the first

ad exponendum ⁊ indocta ad scriben,
dum ea dic ⁊ scribe illa ñ secdin os homi,
nis. nec secdin intellectum humane ad
inuentionis nec secdin uoluntate huma,
ne compositionis ɧ secdin id quod ea in
celestib'desup in mirabilib' dī uides ⁊ au,
dis. ea sic edisserendo proferens quemadmo
dum ⁊ auditor uerba preceptoris sui percipi,
ens. ea secdin tenore locutionis illi' ipso uo
lente. ostendente: ⁊ precipiente proppalat. Sic
q̃ ⁊ tu ó homo. dic ea q̃ uides ⁊ audis ⁊ sc,
be ea non secdin te. nec secdin aliū homi,
nem ɧ secundū uoluntate scientis uiden,
tis ⁊ disponentis omnia in secretis mste,
riorum suorum. Et iterū audiui uoce
de celo michi dicente. Dic q̃ mirabilia
hec. ⁊ scribe ea hoc modo edocta ⁊ dic.

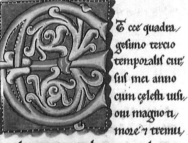

Et ecce quadra,
gesimo tercio
temporalis cur,
sus mei anno
cum celesti uisi,
oni magno ti,
more ⁊ tremu,
la intentione inhererem uidi maxi,
mū splendore. in quo facta ē uox
de celo ad me dicens. O homo fragi,
lis ⁊ cinis cineris ⁊ putredo putredi,
nis. dic ⁊ scribe q̃ uides ⁊ audis. Sed
quia timida es ad loquendū ⁊ simplex

actum ē in millesimo centesimo
quadragesimo primo filii dī ihū xp̄i
incarnationis anno. cū q̃draginta duor̃
annor̃ septē q; mensium eem maxime corusca
tionis igneū lumen apto celo ueniens totū
cerebrū meū transfudit. ⁊ totū cor totūq;
pectus meū uelut flamma ñ tam ar,
dens ɧ calens ita inflammauit. ut sol
rem aliquam calefacit. sup quam radi,
os suos ponit. Et repente intellectum
expositionis libror̃ uidelicet. psalterii
euuangelii ⁊ alior̃ catholicor̃ tam ue,
teris quam noui testamenti uolumi
num sapiebam. ñ autē interpretatio,
nem uerbor̃ textus eor̃ nec diuisione

Figure 2. Hildegard and Volmar (from Prologue to *Scivias*); formerly Wiesbaden,
Hessische Landesbibliothek, ms. 1, folio 1r (lost); copyright Abtei St. Hildegard,
Rüdesheim-Eibingen.

place, given that reassurance was available much closer to home. What is typical, though, is that Hildegard took the initiative here, as she would frequently do in later correspondence, with the letter serving to bring Hildegard to Bernard's attention. The self-promotion inherent therein characterizes much of Hildegard's later activity, and letters were to be a prime medium for the dissemination of her visions. Writing to such an illustrious personage was an auspicious beginning for her engagement with the outside world.

Bernard's reply was short and businesslike: God's grace was in her and she should respond to it. Hildegard's vita, however, allots him a major role in the next stage of her worldly fame (*Vita* 1:4). Between November 30, 1147, and February 13, 1148, the Church held a council on ecclesiastical reforms in Trier, not that far distant from Disibodenberg; both Eugenius III (the first Cistercian pope) and Bernard were in attendance. At just this time, the *Vita* says, the archbishop of Mainz and his senior clergy were examining writings of Hildegard brought to them by Abbot Cuno. Taking advantage of the pope's presence nearby, they let him know about Hildegard, which prompted Eugenius to send a commission to Disibodenberg to examine Hildegard. The commission returned with Hildegard's writings (presumably what had been written so far of *Scivias*), which the pope read aloud. Bernard then urged the pope to validate Hildegard's gift, which Eugenius did (according to the *Vita*) with a letter granting her permission to reveal what she had seen and encouraging her to write everything down. He also composed a congratulatory letter to Abbot Cuno and his monks.

This is a wonderful and dramatic story, with a fairy tale–like quality to it, and would represent the first time a pope had ever given approval for a potentially controversial theological work.[35] But its accuracy is another matter.[36] Letters in the Middle Ages were quasi-public documents, copied, shared, read aloud, and sometimes even revised. No copy survives of either the letter to Hildegard or to the monks; the letter in the Riesencodex that recounts this story is a fabrication. Would Hildegard and her nuns really not have safeguarded this most important letter from the Supreme Pontiff? A letter that, more than any other, saved her from charges of heresy? Quite possibly the *Vita* presents the story of a desired rather than actual past. This scenario of no real letter is made even likelier given a papal charter from February 18, 1148, directly related to Disibodenberg in which the pope provides apostolic protection for the monastery and confirms its property holdings.[37] The charter mentions neither Hildegard nor her writings, despite its suggestive date. Yet neither Bernard nor the pope expressly forbade Hildegard from continuing her work, and this at a time when the Church eagerly pursued perceived heretics. This implies at least a tacit approval of her activity.[38]

Hildegard wrote to the pope around this time (Letter 2). The letter opens with her standard humility topos ("poor little woman though I am"), acknowledges the representatives sent by the pope (asserting that God had "foreordained" them), and mentions that she has sent on some of her writings. Claiming that God has instructed her to write Eugenius, she says she wants the Light of Light to "arouse your spirit to your duty concerning my writings." For the first time we hear that "many people . . . disparage these writings of mine."

No reply to this letter survives, if indeed one ever existed. Hildegard was to write various later letters to Eugenius; he seems to have written only one to her, Letter 4. All of these letters demonstrate the same initiative seen in the letter to Bernard. As she approached the age of fifty, Hildegard was not going to wait for things to come to her. She was going to go after what she wanted.

Nowhere is this clearer than in the aftermath to the Synod of Trier. The *Vita* (1:5) describes a newfound fame following this gathering. It led first to overcrowding of the women's quarters at Disibodenberg via new members of the community—the number of women almost doubled under Hildegard's leadership (her sister Clementia joined her at some point). Then came a new vision of profound impact. Hildegard saw "a place where the river Nahe flows into the Rhine, a hill dedicated in days of old to the name of St Rupert the Confessor."[39] This, she believed, was where God wanted the women's community to move.

Not surprisingly, this vision met with rather less enthusiasm than the one that led to *Scivias*. The monks of Disibodenberg had nothing to gain and everything to lose by the departure of the women. Almost since its founding, their monastery had benefited from the presence of a noted holy woman, first Jutta and then, eventually, Hildegard. Such women were draws for the faithful, whose visits and requests for prayer and intercession would bring gifts—including valuable property—and fame, which led to more gifts and still more fame. Further, women joining a religious community brought with them a dowry. While it was not as large as that given to a husband, it was nonetheless not something a monastery would wish to lose. Thus, from a purely practical point of view, Hildegard's departure would be disastrous for Disibodenberg.

Faced with opposition, Hildegard fell ill, becoming paralyzed and remaining so until the abbot and brothers finally admitted the validity of her vision and acquiesced to her departure, helped along by the intervention of Archbishop Heinrich of Mainz and the Marchioness von Stade, mother of Richardis, Hildegard's favorite nun (*Vita* 2:5). Preparations for the purchase of the abandoned property and for making it hospitable again met with various delays, prompting further illness on Hildegard's part; her health fluctuated in sync with progress toward her goal (*Vita* 1:6). Finally all was ready. Guibert, writing in 1177 while at Rupertsberg and while Hildegard was still alive, says that the convent was founded twenty-seven years previously (1150);[40] a property record from around 1200 says that Hildegard lived at Rupertsberg for thirty years, thus from 1149.[41] Probably in 1149 or 1150, then, Hildegard and her twenty or so women, as well as Volmar, their priest and confessor, moved to their new home on the Rupertsberg, near Bingen on the Rhine.

2 | A New Life

Newfound Freedom

In many ways Hildegard's life at Rupertsberg echoed that of Jutta at Disibodenberg. People came to her in person and wrote to her, asking for her prayers,
advice, and help. She healed the sick, she was sometimes tart in her responses
to letter writers, and her fame continued to spread. At the same time, we cannot
overestimate the differences between life at Rupertsberg and life at Disibodenberg for Hildegard. She and her companions went from a kind of captivity to a
remarkable freedom. One can only imagine what it must have been like for Hildegard to experience the outside world for the first time in almost forty years, to
go from what were cramped living quarters to, in effect, an entire monastery of
her own (even though it was doubtless some years before the site's building and
rebuilding were completed; see figure 3 for a view of Rupertsberg at its height).
Instead of being under the dominion of Abbot Cuno (though technically she
remained so), Hildegard was in charge in terms of both moral leadership and
fiduciary matters. And as we shall see, the entire tenor of the community was
changed. Hildegard was a very different person from Jutta, and she now was
free to act on those differences.

Figure 3. Rupertsberg, from Daniel Meißner and Eberhard Kieser, *Thesaurus Philopoliticus oder Politisches Schatzkästlein* (Frankfurt A.M., 1628), Pars secunda, plate 43; Bayerische Staatsbibliothek München, Mapp. 22-2, 1/2, plate 43, urn:nbn:de:bvb:12-bsb11165552-6.

The difference in physical space was an obvious one. The dimensions of the nuns' living quarters at Disibodenberg are unknown, but if modern conjectures are correct, they would have been a tight fit for the number living there when Hildegard received her traveling vision. That number was either nineteen (*Vita* 1:7) or twenty-one (*Vita* 2:5, an autobiographical portion); in any event, things must have been crowded.

Also significantly different were the surroundings. Rupertsberg was distant from Disibodenberg, making casual contact impossible. Today the thirty-kilometer distance is a twenty-minute drive by autobahn (and by country roads a full hour), and obviously transportation was far slower in the twelfth century. Rupertsberg was built on a much gentler slope than Disibodenberg and was much less isolated. Both sites were at the confluence of two rivers, but Disibodenberg was at the juncture of the Nahe and the Glan whereas Rupertsberg overlooked the Nahe's link to the vastly more important Rhine. And Rupertsberg was just across the Nahe from the busy town of Bingen (whence the name by which Hildegard is known today), while Eibingen lay little more than four kilometers distant on the other side of the Rhine. By contrast, Disibodenberg lacked any nearby town.

The relative openness of Rupertsberg's location was mirrored in the interior life of the community. The nuns at Disibodenberg were enclosed within a male environment, and Jutta had set a model of penitential—arguably extreme—behavior, with a focus on individual virtue. Were there expectations at Disibodenberg that Hildegard should follow that model? The saintly Jutta was a powerful role model for Hildegard, but ultimately a negative one. Perhaps because Hildegard herself experienced illness and suffering that was not self-imposed, she rejected the idea of extreme asceticism, noting that "immoderate abstinence breeds an arrogant boastfulness."[1] At Rupertsberg the nuns were their own community, and moderation—which by definition does not call attention to itself—was the rule. Is it any surprise that although both Jutta and Hildegard were free from the very real dangers of pregnancy and childbirth, the latter lived to be eighty-one while the former died in her mid-forties?

Musical Life

Not the least of the differences between Rupertsberg and Disibodenberg was music. To understand just how different the situation was requires a look at the role of music in Hildegard's life up to this point.

Prior to entering Disibodenberg, she would have heard secular music performed from memory; instrumental accompaniment or any instrumental music would have been improvised. Sacred music, heard in church, would likely have been plainchant only. Complex polyphony was still quite rare in the early twelfth century, and even simple polyphony was possibly unknown in the small parish churches of the Rhineland. Most of all, music would have formed only an occasional part of Hildegard's life when she lived in the secular world.

Monastic communities, on the other hand, led extraordinarily rich musical lives. Communal life consisted of two parts: the *opus mundi*, work of the world, and the *opus dei*, work of God. The *opus mundi* indeed comprised the mundane tasks of existence, incorporating all the work necessary for a self-sustaining rural community. The *opus dei*, on the other hand, was the true purpose of monastic life: the praise of God in a complex and ever changing daily liturgy spun out across the entire year. Every day members of the community would come together to celebrate not just the Mass, the component of the liturgy still most visible in Catholic worship, but also the Divine Office, a series of eight services of varying lengths that incorporated readings, prayers, and other items.

Almost every part of every service was sung, typically in plainchant. Of the many components of the liturgy, the 150 psalms played a prime role, spread out across the day and the week so that each psalm was sung at least once per week. The psalms themselves were chanted to specific "psalm tones," short recitational formulas that could accommodate any amount of text. Each psalm, or sometimes a small group of psalms, was preceded and followed by an antiphon, a distinctive melody sung to a text that specifically fit the feast being celebrated on a given day.

This monastic practice was followed whether the community was one of monks or of nuns. At the time of enclosure or at some point thereafter, Jutta and Hildegard made their monastic professions. They were thus nuns, and, theo- retically at least, responsible for following the liturgical rounds like all professed monastics. In a double monastery in the early twelfth century, that would nor- mally mean singing together with the monks.

What happened at Disibodenberg, however, is open to debate. Initially, at least, it hardly seems possible that Hildegard and the two Juttas would have left their enclosure to join the monks for services, and a statement by Guibert decades later indicates that they had "access . . . to the offices of the monks at their psalm- ody nearby."[2] In other words, the monks performed the Divine Office that the women overheard (the exact location of the enclosure is currently unknown).

Hildegard's becoming *magistra* at Disibodenberg and the addition of still more women to her community may have led to a change in full enclosure and, perhaps briefly, to the opportunity to sing along with the monks (a scenario for which no evidence exists, however). But if so, that commingling didn't last; the Second Lateran Council forbade the practice in 1139. Thus, when Hildegard got to Rupertsberg, she likely either would never have sung in a real church with real acoustics (if enclosure had been strict), or it would have been years since she had done so.

Although music was only one of Hildegard's creative ventures, it was of extraordinary significance to her. The two likeliest scenarios we can imagine for her musical life at Disibodenberg both involve a restriction of some kind: either the requirement that she and her fellow nuns remain silent while the monks sang in services, or the musical constraints demanded by observing the Divine Office in their own cramped quarters. Given Hildegard's firm belief in the symbolic importance of music (which she wrote about late in life), and what must surely have been a personal passion for it, life at Disibodenberg could not have provided much musical satisfaction. The need to create music (an autobiographical portion of the *Vita* places Hildegard's first compositions during her time at Disiboden- berg[3]) and the desire for musical freedom were surely among the reasons she felt impelled to burst the bonds that tied her to the monastery where she had lived for almost forty years—even if these reasons were subconscious and not articulated.

With freedom—musical and otherwise—came enormous responsibility and an initial set of problems that took years to solve. Hildegard and her nuns had left an established, flourishing monastery with "a lushness of fields and vineyards" for "an arid place with no conveniences," as she put it in the *Vita*.[4] At the time of their arrival at Rupertsberg, their financial situation was precarious, and their precise relationship to Disibodenberg was still a matter of contention. Hildegard's unwavering belief in her mission—God's mission, rather—sustained her through the eight-odd years that it took to put the new monastery on a firm footing.

A Rededication

One of the earliest events at Rupertsberg for which we have a record is the reconsecration of the church. On May 1, no later than (and probably in) 1151, Archbishop Heinrich of Mainz rededicated the church—perhaps only a chapel at that early date—to Mary, apostles Philip and James, and confessors Martin and Rupert.[5] While at Rupertsberg the archbishop also received the monastic vows of some young women and, very helpfully, gave the new foundation a mill property, noting that Rupertsberg lacked its own mill. Hildegard may have been involved in plans for the church that arose on the Rupertsberg, just as other ecclesiastics of the time were (e.g., Abbot Suger with Saint-Denis); architecture plays an important role in the third part of *Scivias*, written at just the time that at least some building would have been going on.[6]

The dedicatees of the church were also dedicatees of some of Hildegard's music. She wrote compositions for both apostles and confessors (as groups), as well as (not surprisingly) St. Rupert himself. Mary was an especial focus of Hildegard's attention; while typical for a time during which Marian worship flourished, Hildegard's interest in Mary also reflects a personal theology that has many female-centric components.[7] Possibly some of the works for these dedicatees originated in connection with this important ceremony; the sequence for St. Rupert, *O ierusalem aurea civitas*, has been suggested as being for this occasion.

Four other, different compositions have a potential connection as well. Three are shorter compositions: Hildegard's Kyrie and two antiphons for the dedication of a church, *O orzchis ecclesia* and *O choruscans lux stellarum*.[8] The last is her play with music, *Ordo virtutum*.

O orzchis ecclesia is a very unusual piece. It is not an especially long work, and it is in Hildegard's favorite mode, E. It is designated in the Riesencodex as being for the dedication of a church, and the text, by Hildegard (as is true for all of her compositions save the Kyrie) can easily be read as referring to the ceremony of church dedication:[9] O immense church / girded with divine armor and dressed with jacinth / you are the aroma of the stigmata of the people / and the city of knowledge / o o you are also anointed in high sound / and are a glittering gem.[10] The reference to "the city of knowledge" would also be especially meaningful for Hildegard, for as we shall see, she proceeded to create such an atmosphere at Rupertsberg. What is unusual about the song is its incorporation of five made-up words, the only example we have of practical use of Hildegard's own *Lingua ignota*. A second, possibly related work for a church dedication is *O choruscans lux stellarum*, which also provides a glowing description of the church and likens it as well to "a glittering gem." Perhaps it was composed about the same time as *O orzchis ecclesia*, as a straightforward companion for that song without the invented words. A third work suggested is Hildegard's Kyrie, discussed in detail in chapter 9. This was a versatile work that was sung in daily Mass and was also part of three components of the daily Divine Office. It also serves as part of the ceremony for the dedication of a church.[11] Indeed, in the Riesencodex it is copied immediately after the four antiphons for the dedication of a church and is in fact side by side with *O orzchis ecclesia* in the manuscript's double-column layout.

Hildegard's remaining two works for the dedication of a church—*O virgo ecclesia* and *Nunc gaudeant materna viscera*—cannot be firmly pinned down. They read as a pair, with the former lamenting how a savage wolf has snatched the Church's children and referring to the cunning serpent. In *Nunc gaudeant* it is time to rejoice, as the children have been returned and the serpent confounded. Although the papal schism that began in 1159 might at first seem a possible inspiration, *Nunc gaudeant* appears in the so-called Dendermonde manuscript, copied before the end of the schism in 1177. Another theory holds that the two works refer to the revolt of the radical reformer Arnold of Brescia, who was driven out of Rome during Holy Week of 1155.[12] Hildegard certainly would not have been a supporter of Arnold, who preached against the Church establishment and forced the pope to flee Rome.

Ordo virtutum

The other work possibly performed in connection with the reconsecration of the Rupertsberg church is the *Ordo virtutum*. Hildegard's most substantial work by far is this dramatic work with music. The title is most often translated as "The Play of the Virtues." Although "ordo" means series, row, line, or order in classical

Latin, during the Middle Ages the term was used for both dramas (e.g., the *Ordo prophetarum)* and liturgical ceremonies (e.g., the *Ordo Romanus*). The final vision of *Scivias* includes a shorter version of the text alone; this was likely a reshaping of the full drama rather than the first version of the work, as some believe.[13]

The play is not divided into formal acts but suggests a series of logical subdivisions, and modern editions of both text and music typically organize the work into acts and scenes. Except for certain important sections, the work is sung throughout in a series of eighty-seven individual songs. In the Riesencodex each song and the character singing are indicated by rubrication (the use of red text).

The play opens with a quasi-prologue. Patriarchs and Prophets ask, "Who are these, who are like clouds?" and are answered by the Virtues. Patriarchs and Prophets then sing again, beginning with "We are the roots and you are the branches," to bring the prologue to a close.

The action of the play opens with embodied souls, lamenting that they are sinners. They are answered by Anima ("Soul"), who invokes the Virtues. She is referred to in various ways throughout the play: *felix* (happy), *gravata* (burdened), *infelix* (unhappy), *querela* (lamenting), and *penitens* (penitent). Anima begins happily, but as her dialogue with the Virtues unfolds, she becomes progressively less happy as she details her difficulty in fighting against her body. After the first named Virtue, Knowledge of God, informs Anima that she doesn't know, see, or taste the one who made her, she responds that God made the world and that wanting to enjoy it doesn't harm him.

At this point the Devil makes his dramatic entrance. The entrance is dramatic for two reasons. The first is the word applied to his entrance: "strepitus" (noise, din, racket, crash, etc.). In other words, his is a loud arrival on the scene. Even more striking, though, is that the Devil's role is a speaking one; in contrast to everyone else in the play, he never gets to sing. Thus, many decades before Hildegard outlined her musical manifesto in a letter to the prelates of Mainz, her art embodied her philosophy: the devil hates music.

The Devil lets Anima know that the world is ready to embrace her "with great honor." It is not Anima who responds to him, however, but the Virtues. The Devil taunts them by saying that they don't even know who they are, but this taunt leads to the central section of the play, which focuses on the individual Virtues. Each introduces herself in turn, "Ego Humilitas" (I, Humility), "Ego Karitas" (I, Charity), and so on, explaining what she stands for to a supportive response from the other Virtues.

The Virtues are seventeen in number: Knowledge of God, Humility (who calls herself "Queen of the Virtues"), Charity, Fear of God, Obedience, Faith,

Hope, Chastity, Innocence, Contempt of the World, Heavenly Love, Modesty, Mercy, Victory, Discretion, Patience, and one unnamed Virtue (modern writers have suggested "Discipline" and "Heavenly Desire" as possible names).

At some point during this scene Anima disappears, along with the Devil, for after each Virtue has sung her part, all join to lament and mourn their lost sheep. Anima then reappears, now penitent, lamenting her sins and calling on the Virtues to assist her. Back and forth they go, with Anima begging for help (including an interspersed German "ach! ach!") and the Virtues urging her to be strong, telling her that God will take her back. The Virtues declare that heaven will rejoice in her return and that "it is fitting for us to resound 'in symphonia.'"

As soon as Anima and the Virtues are reconciled, the Devil returns. He cries that he will bring Anima down, but she fires back that she will fight him and calls on Humility for aid. Humility, Victory, Chastity, and the other Virtues then capture and bind the Devil. The *Ordo* concludes with an evocation of creation ("In the beginning all creation was green"), presumably sung by all forces, ending with the exhortation for all to genuflect to God the Father, who will reach out to them.

The performing forces for *Ordo virtutum* were likely carefully chosen. The seventeen Virtues and Anima could be sung by eighteen women, almost exactly the number Hildegard had with her when she moved to Rupertsberg. The embodied souls could have been sung by the nuns as well, or any nuns not assigned a specific role, with Volmar as the Devil. This leaves the Patriarchs and Prophets, a role possibly sung by the dignitaries visiting at the time the Rupertsberg church was reconsecrated (if that was indeed the first time the work was performed).

As in any drama, the parts are not distributed equally. The combined parts of the Virtues far exceed anything else (thirty-six sections). The embodied souls have a single section, though one that is comparatively long (just over five lines in the Riesencodex). The Patriarchs and Prophets sing two sections, but each is quite short: a single line to open the work, and a mere two lines for their second bit. These short parts could easily have been learned by visitors.

Of the solo parts, Anima's is the longest, with a dozen sections of more than thirty-two lines total. Thirteen of the Virtues are assigned a single utterance, ranging in substance from a single line (Innocence) to four lines (Contemptus Mundi). Humilitas, Castitas, Victoria, and Scientia Dei (Humility, Chastity, Victory, and Knowledge of God) have multiple sections: two for Scientia Dei (each barely two lines long), three each for Castitas and Victoria (a total of thirteen and six lines, respectively), and eight parts for Humilitas (about nineteen lines total). The closing tutti is by far the most substantial unit of the whole work, at fourteen lines; Hildegard clearly recognized the need for an appropriate conclusion.

Aside from the last section, then, the work consists of a series of mostly short units, each of which is internally coherent. Indeed, modern performers have sometimes recorded individual units of *Ordo virtutum* separately. The overall style is one of generally limited range; fifty-eight of the sections have the range of a ninth or less (thus, much less than the normal range for one of Hildegard's songs). As noted, most of the parts are short as well, and syllabic text setting is common. E and D modes are dominant throughout (see the discussion on mode in chapter 8), and Hildegard deploys her changing modal centers carefully to delineate characterization and drama.[14]

Deviations from this basic style thus stand out, and Hildegard uses moments of musical symbolism throughout (some examples appear below). Although the overall range of the work is two octaves, only one singer explores the entire range: Victory. Appropriately enough, Victory is also allotted one of the only two appearances of the highest pitch in the work (the other, interestingly, goes to Mercy). The lowest note, by contrast, is ubiquitous.

Victory and Mercy are also the only two soloists who use C mode, a mode that appears in the *Ordo* toward the conclusion of the important "Virtues" section and then again in Victory's final speech, where she calls on her companions to rejoice now that the Devil has been bound. Thus, even though Victory's total singing time is not extensive, Hildegard has indicated her importance through range, mode, and the placement of her solos.

Chastity's significance is marked musically as well, not surprisingly given Hildegard's extolling of virginity throughout her writings. Chastity's initial song is the longest sung by any of the Virtues so far in *Ordo* (five lines), and is equalled by only one other Virtue, Contemptus Mundi (Contempt of the World). Chastity's other two pieces are placed in an extremely important position in the drama. The Devil has been bound, and Chastity is the one who "chastises" him. The Devil responds, mocking Chastity's lack of sexual knowledge and thus fertility, but Chastity answers by identifying herself with Mary and reminding the Devil that Mary's fecundity brought forth the one who would destroy him. Each of these last two pieces is given the relatively wide range of an eleventh (of the Virtues, only Victory has a wider range; Humility, Hope, and—interestingly—Modesty also reach an eleventh).

As noted above, the embodied souls have a relatively substantial composition to sing. Positioned as the first piece after the prologue, their words identify them as pilgrims, but sinful ones. Hildegard lays out standard elements of her writing here, noting the inheritance lost through Adam and asking for God's help. The length devoted to this part is fitting, given the theme of the entire play and the overwhelming likelihood that it was written for her nuns. Symbolically, the singers are constrained in their range as well, as the piece is confined to an octave.

Anima's two longest speeches, respectively about four and six lines, take place after her return from her sojourn in the world. The first, her initial utterance on return, is taken up predominantly by her description and praise of the Virtues ("O you regal Virtues, how beautiful and how shining you are!") Anima's highest note in the entire *Ordo* is reached here, with text-painting for the word "summo," literally "highest." To the nun singing this part, this section would easily stand out, for it lies a full fourth higher than anywhere else in her role. The second long piece provides Anima's fullest statement of her position: "I am the sinner . . . incline toward me . . . and help me."

Although the Virtues as a group are usually limited to relatively short responses to others' speeches, in a few instances they make longer statements. In the section where each Virtue introduces herself and the grouped Virtues respond, the longest response is the one following Chastity's introduction—yet another marking by Hildegard of Chastity's prominence. Still longer speeches appear elsewhere in the play. The first is, appropriately, the Virtues' response to the Devil's initial appearance. In a parallel placement, the second occurs right before the return of the Devil, as the Virtues rejoice at the return of Anima and their reconciliation ("O living fountain, how great is your sweetness!"). In the last, once again, the Virtues follow a speech by Chastity.

The combination of dramatic differences in the length and ranges of individual parts and the close correspondence between the number of nuns in Hildegard's community and the number of solo parts virtually guarantees that Hildegard wrote the work with specific singers in mind. The very short part of Innocence, for example, suggests a younger, less experienced (and possibly self-effacing) singer, while Anima would likely have been for someone with both vocal confidence and a certain amount of presence. Which part, then, would Hildegard have sung? That she merely sat on the sidelines and watched is inconceivable. The likeliest role is that of Humility, which is not as ironic as it might sound. In all of Hildegard's writings, she repeatedly stresses her role as that of a small, weak vessel through whom God chose to reveal his truths. Of all the individual Virtues, Humility sings most frequently, and she is the one to whom Anima and the other Virtues look for guidance. She is the first to respond individually to the Devil, and in her "I, Humility" song she calls on the Virtues to come to her (in their response, they "come willingly"). She is the one who concludes the important section where the Virtues identify themselves individually; she is the one who instructs the Virtues to receive Anima again in their fold. She commands Victory to head with her "knights" to bind the Devil, and she repeats her demand to all the Virtues.[15] The role suits Hildegard's take-charge personality perfectly, and her assuming of it would serve as an unspoken reminder of the necessity for her nuns to follow and obey her in the still precarious situation of the newly established Rupertsberg. Indeed, we know that not all of her original cohort (including, most conspicuously, Richardis) chose to stay at Rupertsberg, so dramatizing the need for obedience was by no means superfluous.

The eighty-seven individual short pieces of *Ordo virtutum* add up to Hildegard's longest musical work. Sometimes thought to represent an abstraction rather than something that would have been performed, the work was surely intended for performance and has received numerous modern productions in Europe and North America.[16] Although the work is presented in the manuscripts without staging or similar information (as is normal for medieval drama), Hildegard's description of the Virtues in *Scivias* can offer clues as to how some of them could have been costumed. In the opening of vision 8 of part 3, Humility (here again in first place), Charity, Fear of God, Obedience, Faith, Hope, and Chastity are all present with their attire described. Humility, for example, "wore a golden crown on her head, with three higher prongs; it was radiantly adorned with green and red precious stones and white pearls. On her breast she had a shining mirror, in which appeared with wondrous brightness the image of the incarnate Son of God."[17] Such a costume may sound extreme, and perhaps Hildegard's nuns only approximated this vision, but we will soon see that Hildegard's nuns did, indeed, wear gold crowns on special occasions. And the visual representations of the Virtues in *Scivias* are evidently of great importance to Hildegard, for she returns to them over and over in vision 8 of part 3. Clothing and accessories are described upon initial introduction of the Virtues (opening through section 7), again in section 17 ("On the appearance and dress of the aforesaid virtues and what it means"), and yet again individually in sections 18 through 25 (section 18, "Humility and her appearance"; section 19, "Charity and her appearance"; and so on). After having attached this much symbolic import to the visual representation of the Virtues in *Scivias*, Hildegard likely drew upon at least some of these cues for costuming in *Ordo virtutum*.

Hildegard's play was not written in a vacuum. The roots of medieval liturgical drama date back to the ninth century, though it flourished most prominently in the thirteenth century. Disibodenberg may even have put on a liturgical drama; a manuscript from either the monastery itself or nearby included one.[18]

Because the subject matter of *Ordo virtutum* is not related to a biblical tale, unlike surviving liturgical dramas, it is often considered instead a morality play, and even the first of that genre by a good two centuries. *Ordo virtutum*, though, differs from later morality plays in the structure of the cast, the absence of death, the offstage relegation of sin, and the fact that later plays are much earthier than Hildegard's philosophically oriented drama.[19] It differs from other music dramas of the Middle Ages in eschewing any plot derivation from the Bible, saints' lives, or miracle tales (it is also unique in having a named author; all other plays, at least from the twelfth century, are anonymous).

One (controversial) suggestion is that *Ordo virtutum* reflects Hildegard's knowledge of the drama *Dulcitius* by the tenth-century German playwright Hrotsvitha of Gandersheim.[20] More properly, *Ordo virtutum* is influenced by the *Ordo prophetarum* tradition (with declamations on Christ's birth by various prophets), and what Hildegard's work most closely resembles, in fact, is the Latin play *Psychomachia* by fourth-century writer Prudentius, which uses personifications of the virtues to depict the struggle for a virtuous life.[21] As usual, Hildegard would never identify any nonbiblical model for her work, but the strong similarity confirms yet again that she knew and used works by earlier authors as catalysts for her creativity. *Ordo virtutum* differs from *Psychomachia*, however, in the role of the Devil, the status of God as the creator of the world, and the absence of corresponding Vices. As ever, Hildegard shapes her material to her own ends.[22]

Hildegard's fascination with the Virtues was not restricted to *Ordo virtutum*. All of the play's virtues appear in *Scivias*, scattered throughout in various combinations, and *Scivias* includes virtues that are not part of *Ordo virtutum*. In vision 6 of part 3, for example, we encounter Abstinence, Liberality, Piety, Truth, Peace, Beatitude, and Salvation. Again, Hildegard describes their appearance in detail (section 27: "On the virtues' clothing and what it means"; section 28: "Abstinence and her appearance"; and so on).

Even after *Scivias* and *Ordo virtutum*, Hildegard remained committed to exploring the virtues. Her second main theological treatise, *Liber vite meritorum*, provides an even more detailed examination of even more virtues, this time with corresponding vices, and virtues also play a role in Hildegard's commentary on the Benedictine Rule, her homilies on the Gospels, some of her letters, and the *Liber divinorum operum*. And even with the inspiration of *Psychomachia*, *Ordo virtutum* was part of a well-established medieval fascination with vices and virtues.

Widespread medieval interest in the virtues notwithstanding, modern readers have applied a wide range of interpretations to the *Ordo virtutum* and the rationale behind its creation. In addition to the idea that *Ordo virtutum* was written to mark the reconsecration of Rupertsberg's church, it could be a reflection of Hildegard's criticism of the Cathar movement, deemed heretical in her day;[23] a celebration of obedience following revolt;[24] a calling to and celebration of virginity to be performed before the Mass for Consecration of Virgins (because of parallels to the ordo for Consecration in the Mainz Pontifical that Hildegard's community would have used);[25] or a "lyrical celebration of Hildegard's monastic ideal."[26] Half the Virtues could represent the gifts of the Holy Spirit, the other half the Beatitudes,[27] or the play could serve as preparation for sacramental union with Christ.[28] The play may have been anticipated in Hildegard's vision of Jutta's soul following the latter's death or originated in connection with the dedication of the chapel of Mary Magdalene at Disibodenberg in 1142.[29] The contemporary treatise *Speculum virginum* might have influenced its creation.[30] And so on.

Regardless of the original impetus for *Ordo virtutum*, the play was not necessarily confined to a single performance. It is appropriate for many things, including both the dedication of a church and nuns' taking of the veil (both of which occurred in May 1151), and could easily serve for anniversaries of such events. And certainly women continued to join Hildegard's community.

3 | New Challenges

Richardis

One of the most painful experiences of Hildegard's life happened not that long after the nuns were settled in Rupertsberg. Her favorite member of her Benedictine community was noblewoman Richardis von Stade, who had come to Disibodenberg because Jutta was one of her relatives (Jutta's great-grandfather was Richardis's great-great-grandfather). In 1151 Richardis was chosen to be abbess of a monastery in Bassum in northern Germany, far from Rupertsberg but much closer to Stade itself. Richardis's selection was a blow to Hildegard. She would lose her closest female companion and a faithful helper, and Richardis—someone who had previously been subservient to Hildegard—would outrank her within the Church hierarchy. Bassum was a well-established and much better endowed monastery than Rupertsberg, and its leader was an abbess. This was a title that Hildegard herself never held, being technically only a *magistra* subject to the abbot of Disibodenberg.[1]

Richardis was not the only nun who wished to leave Rupertsberg; another was her niece Adelheid, also offered an abbacy. The initially harsh conditions led still others to give up (*Vita* 2:5), but there surely must have been an "et tu, Brute" quality to Richardis's desire to leave. And Hildegard was not about to surrender without a fight. She launched a vigorous letter-writing campaign to prevent Richardis's departure, contacting the two individuals with the strongest personal and spiritual authority over Richardis. One was her mother, who would die later that year (Letter 323, notable for Hildegard's powerful rhetorical repetition: "this position of Abbess that you desire for them is surely, surely, surely not God's will"). The other was Pope Eugenius (the letter does not survive). That missive prompted the pope's only letter to Hildegard that we know of (Letter 4); he noted that Hildegard's reputation had spread far, but rather than getting involved in the dispute, he simply delegated the matter to Hildegard's superior, Archbishop Heinrich of Mainz. Heinrich then commanded Hildegard to release Richardis (Letter 18), but she refused, claiming that God did not want that (Letter 18r). Richardis left anyway (whether in 1151 or 1152 is not known), which prompted a very unhappy letter from Hildegard to Hartwig, who was both archbishop of Bremen and Richardis's brother (Letter 12, with the specter of simony—the selling of ecclesiastical offices—thrown in), and an equally sorrowful one to Richardis herself, asking, literally, why she had forsaken her, using the biblical quotation (Letter 64).[2] This letter is an extremely unusual one for Hildegard. She calls herself "mother" and Richardis "daughter," adopting their former roles at Rupertsberg, but more unusually she actually refers to herself by name. Everywhere else in her voluminous correspondence she speaks as God's emissary; here she speaks as an earthly individual, bereft of what she loves.

The sad conclusion to the story comes in 1152, when Hartwig wrote to Hildegard again, announcing the death of Richardis on October 29 (Letter 13). Pointedly taking care to refer to them by their different titles ("Richardis abbatisse" and "Hildegardi magistre"), Hartwig indicated that in her last confession Richardis "tearfully expressed her longing for your cloister with her whole heart" and that "if death had not prevented, she would have come to you as soon as she was able to get permission."[3] Hildegard replied magnanimously (Letter 13r, where Richardis is "like a flower in her beauty and loveliness in the symphony of this world,") and in one sense she had "won"; God obviously didn't want Richardis at Bassum either. But on a large scale, and very publicly, Hildegard had to submit to forces she could not control—a public loss of face at a vulnerable time not far into her residence at Rupertsberg.

The matter of Richardis has led to two interesting and controversial interpretations of Hildegard's life at this time. One sees *Ordo virtutum* as a reaction by Hildegard to Richardis's desertion: a celebration of obedience following revolt, with Richardis's departure as the generating force.[4] In this view, Richardis is represented by Anima, who is tempted by the glories of the world (leading a rich abbey) but comes to regret her decision and returns to the Virtues who formerly nourished her. Intriguing as this idea is, it's unlikely to be the prompt behind *Ordo virtutum*, given that the derived version of the play appears in *Scivias*, which Hildegard says was finished in 1151 (and thus *Ordo virtutum* itself finished before that). A similar chronological problem dogs the hypothesis that Richardis's death (1152) generated *Ordo virtutum*.[5]

The other take on Hildegard's life, far more controversial, posits an actual love relationship between Hildegard and Richardis.[6] Such an idea is distasteful to those who see Hildegard primarily as a spiritual leader for whom such a relationship would be anathema; it is embraced readily by others who have no difficulty interpreting this as the twelfth-century equivalent of same-sex desire. The coexistence of two such completely opposite views is typical of the way that Hildegard is read by modern audiences.

New Manuscripts

Although Pope Eugenius commented on how well known Hildegard had become, her failure to retain Richardis underscored the limits of her influence. It is unlikely to be a coincidence that the years immediately after Richardis's death saw the appearance of many new creations by Hildegard as well as the beginning of the manuscript dissemination of her writings; these could only help to bolster her reputation. By 1153 a priest from Reutlingen had written that he wished to make a copy of *Scivias* (Letter 187), and at least one collection of Hildegard's letters was under way. Manuscripts for both Hildegard's music and her other writings were typically generated either at Rupertsberg or at places that had close connections with Hildegard personally. Her community was hardly alone in its manuscript production; other women's houses of the time produced attractive volumes, and Disibodenberg itself generated numerous manuscripts.[7]

The copies of Hildegard's works and her many new creations (discussed below) served purposes other than establishing her authority through spreading her version of God's word. They helped to recreate the monastic library that she left behind on leaving Disibodenberg (the year after Jutta's death "much copying of manuscripts" apparently took place there[8]), and in doing so they furnished a foundation for the spiritual education and guidance of Hildegard's nuns. They also helped distinguish her still further from Jutta by both the fact of their production and the outward direction of Hildegard's energies that they embody. Hildegard was by no means the only learned or creative woman of her time—Héloise and the slightly later Herrad of Landsberg come immediately to mind—but no other woman was so consistently productive across as many realms.

Tenxwind

News of Hildegard and her activities did not meet with universal approval. A famous critique comes from a woman known as Tenxwind, or Tengswich, the superior of a foundation of Augustinian canonesses in Andernach, about halfway between Bingen and Cologne along the Rhine (Augustinian foundations were becoming popular for women in the twelfth-century Rhineland). Begun in 1129, Tenxwind's community grew to one hundred women in less than a decade, created illuminated manuscripts, and enjoyed newly composed music. Hers was thus a culturally thriving community.[9]

In a deliciously snide message (Letter 52), Tenxwind, in the guise of innocent inquiry, denounces practices Hildegard is said to be following. Her letter gives us an important glimpse into life under Hildegard. The letter's date is uncertain, but it surely originated after the move to Rupertsberg, since the practices it describes seem unlikely to have been permitted at Disibodenberg. Since Tenxwind died around 1152, it means that Hildegard got a rapid start on making her convent one that was very special.

Tenxwind has heard that

> on feast days your virgins stand in the church with unbound hair when singing the psalms and that as part of their dress they wear white, silk veils, so long that they touch the floor. Moreover, it is said that they wear crowns of gold filigree, into which are secured crosses on both sides and the back, with a figure of the Lamb on the front, and that they adorn their fingers with golden rings. . . . Moreover, that which seems no less strange to us is the fact that you admit into your community only those women from noble, well-established families and absolutely reject others who are of lower birth and of less wealth.[10]

Hildegard responds in her sternest and most formal fashion, not as herself, of course, but in a pronouncement from "The Living Fountain" (Letter 52r). She defends both her nuns' appearance and the favoring of the wealthy—the former by reason of the virginity of her charges, who, unlike married women, are not commanded to hide their beauty; the latter because it is God who establishes and desires ranks on earth. In respect to favoring the nobility, Hildegard is acting both very much as a member of her class and as a Benedictine, the most venerable monastic order and one that welcomed rather than eschewed the advantages that money could bring to a community. In terms of her nuns' appearance, however, her practice appears to be unique.

The crowns, unbound hair, veils, and jewels show up elsewhere in Hildegard's world. Diadems and long hair are found in various of the illuminations (e.g., *Scivias* 2:3, 4, 5, 6; *Liber divinorum operum* 3:3). In that last vision one of those wearing a diadem is Humility herself, keeping with Hildegard's claim of appropriate attire.[11] In the miniature for *Scivias* 2:5, women wear shimmering veils as well, and Hildegard's description of the vision goes into detail about the attire of virgins: "wonderfully adorned with gold and gems"; "heads veiled in white, adorned with a gold circlet"; "on their foreheads the Lamb of God."[12] She is clearly describing her own practice, revealed to her in a vision. In *Liber vite meritorum*, beautiful clothing, crowns, and jewels are among the joys of heaven (Part 6: 25–30).

The story of the crowns spread further afield; in 1175 the monk Guibert of Gembloux, later to play a key role in Hildegard's life, wrote her a letter of inquiry that included (among other things) the questions "Is it by divine revelation or merely for the sake of ornamentation that you have your virgins wear crowns? And further, how are we to interpret the distinctions among the various crowns, for we have heard that they are not all the same?" (Letter 103). Hildegard responded that "I . . . had a vision about crowns. I saw that all the orders of the church have distinct emblems according to their celestial brightness, but that virginity has no such distinguishing emblem save the black veil and the sign of the cross. And I saw that a white veil to cover a virgin's head was to be the proper emblem of virginity. For this veil stands for the white garment which man once had, but subsequently lost, in Paradise" (Letter 103r). She goes on to explain in detail how the circlet on the virgin's head represents the Trinity.

Around 1230 the nuns at Rupertsberg created a beautiful altar cloth that included a depiction of Hildegard. On it she has a halo (a nod to her desired canonization) and is wearing a white veil; the tradition, or at least the memory of it, lasted for fifty years after her death.[13] Hildegard's own crown and veil ended up in Trier.[14]

The picture of crown, veil, and jewelry is certainly a fascinating one, and it is in keeping with Hildegard's visual orientation. She is someone who literally saw things; she is believed to have played an important role in creating the artwork that accompanies her writings; she invented the distinctive shapes of a new alphabet; her texts are filled with arresting images; and her musical notation even uses symbols not found elsewhere. For her nuns to look different as well fits with this overall picture.

Elisabeth of Schönau

A complete contrast to Tenxwind's letter is the first one sent by Elisabeth of Schönau (Letter 201), like Hildegard both nun and visionary. Somewhat younger than Hildegard, she lived on the other side of the Rhine, not that far from Rupertsberg. Elisabeth writes to Hildegard seeking support for her own visions, which have not been well received. Hildegard responds (Letter 201r), writing as a "fragile vessel" for the "Serene Light," with theological explanations as to why visionaries are necessary and why they must remain humble.

Elisabeth was not merely a younger visionary; she was very likely the catalyst for one of Hildegard's most extensive groups of compositions: the thirteen compositions in honor of St. Ursula and her 11,000 Virgins. Only the Virgin Mary received more attention from Hildegard in her music. In addition to eight interrelated antiphons, Ursula (and her companions, in some pieces) garnered the hymn *Cum vox sanguinis*, the sequence *O ecclesia*, the Gospel antiphon *O rubor sanguinis*, and two responsories, *Favus distillans* and *Spiritui sancto honor sit*.

Hildegard's interest in Ursula was not necessarily the result of a desire to highlight a female saint but rather reflected Ursula's prominence in the twelfth-century Rhineland. In 1106 a cemetery dating to Roman times was discovered in Cologne, and the bones therein were believed to be those of Ursula and her companions. In 1143, while Hildegard was still there, Disibodenberg received relics from three of the 11,000 Virgins,[15] and Rupertsberg eventually received a relic as well.[16] The identification with Ursula and companions, though, was questioned in 1156, after the discovery that the gravesite included the bones of men, not just those of women.

Shortly thereafter, in 1156–1157, Elisabeth of Schönau's visions provided the explanation for this commingling of the sexes. According to Elisabeth, the bones of men found in the Cologne graves were those of the devout bishops who were martyred along with Ursula and her companions. The book of Elisabeth's Ursula visions circulated very widely, with more than seventy manuscript copies still extant, and Hildegard's Ursula compositions acknowledge Elisabeth's revelations. Her antiphon *De patria etiam earum*, for example, addresses the presence of men directly.

Hildegard makes the sequence *O ecclesia* the longest work of her set (thirty lines; the hymn *Cum vox sanguinis* is twenty-six) and the one that uses the widest range (a thirteenth; *Cum vox sanguinis* reaches a twelfth). The text again employs Hildegard's rich images, but with a dissonant note, as Ursula is mocked by those who do not understand her "vision of true faith." The parallels with Hildegard's own life, especially in the 1150s while the independence, legitimacy, and financial foundations of Rupertsberg were still being established, is unmistakable, and Hildegard even uses similar language when she describes her own move.[17] Interestingly, Hildegard uses the word "symphonia" twice in this song, once when Ursula is being mocked "in great harmony" (in magna symphonia) and at the end, when all the heavens praise the Lamb of God "in highest harmony" (in summa symphonia). One more striking appearance in the text is the German word "wach," a cry of woe from all the elements that observe the slaughter of Ursula and her companions. The interjection of German—Hildegard's native tongue—into her music is extremely rare and reserved for very special places (it also appears in *Ordo virtutum*).

Financial Independence

An important issue facing Hildegard after her move to Rupertsberg was her community's financial and spiritual independence. The reluctance of Abbot Cuno and the brothers of Disibodenberg to loosen ties with the women did not evaporate on the nuns' departure. Instead, most of the 1150s were concerned with determining just what the relationship between Rupertsberg and Disibodenberg was to be. Interactions between the two communities were none too positive, nor did they improve on the death of Cuno (July 2, 1155) and the appointment of his successor Helenger (July 17). For a high-profile ecclesiastic to leave—a woman, at that—was a serious blow to the amour propre of the monastery. At one point (the precise date is unknown) Hildegard returned to Disibodenberg to try to resolve the issues, after first, as usual, undergoing a period of illness. Her reception was unpleasant: "A mob of . . . monks rose up and gnashed their teeth at me, as if I were a bird of gloom or a horrid beast" (Letter 75).[18] She nonetheless ceded them most of the possessions given to Disibodenberg when various nuns had joined that community, and she even gave them money to stop their complaints (*Vita* 1:7), though warning them not to attempt to take Volmar away from Rupertsberg.[19]

Poor relations between the two communities did not prevent Cuno from seeking Hildegard's visionary assistance. His request was straightforward: "I ask that you impart to me any revelation God has granted you concerning our patron, the blessed Disibod" (Letter 74). Hildegard's response has her usual chastisement as to the foolishness of the one who had contacted her. Copies of the letter also include the texts for three songs about the saint: the antiphon *O mirum admirandum*, the responsory *O viriditas digiti dei*, and the spectacular sequence *O presul vere civitatis*. These, though, may not have been part of her original response, thus leaving open their date of composition.[20]

It was not until 1158 that a final legal agreement was reached. Two charters from Archbishop Arnold of Mainz, dated May 22 of that year, confirm the property and possessions now owned by Rupertsberg, indicate that the abbot of Disibodenberg must provide the priest necessary for their community and cannot remove him without approval of the nuns (i.e., Volmar was to stay at Rupertsberg), and give the women the right to choose Hildegard's successor "in free election according to the Rule of blessed Benedict."[21] The economic independence of Rupertsberg is firmly established (among other things, Disibodenberg keeps the nuns' original dowries but relinquishes eight houses instead), and Rupertsberg is placed under the protection of the archdiocese. It was, in general, a victory for Hildegard.

4 | New Creations

The signing of the charters brought the earliest period at Rupertsberg to a close, and Hildegard then embarked on her second big theological treatise, the *Liber vite meritorum*. The preface to that book, written after she had finished the treatise, is of great importance by itself, for we learn what Hildegard did creatively between her arrival at Rupertsberg and the start of *Liber vite meritorum*. After bringing *Scivias* to its conclusion in 1151, she generated a series of smaller works in wildly different genres, discussed below, and only then returned to writing a major theological work. What we see, then, is a pattern of creation that is eminently sensible. The move to Rupertsberg, in essence, opened the floodgates. It hardly seems surprising that it was only after Hildegard's move that she was able to complete *Scivias*. Yet it is still impressive that she was able to bring this work to conclusion in the midst of what must have been many demands on her time, facing problems that would have been unknown to her at Disibodenberg. That the next works after *Scivias* were smaller in scope was surely owing to a combination of factors. The time spent on solving problems meant that (relatively) shorter rather than longer works were in order, and there was doubtless need for a kind of intellectual respite; none of the other works from the 1150s tackles issues in the depth found in *Scivias*. But the wide variety of works that led up to *Liber vite meritorum* were all touched by Hildegard's theological message in various ways, and they served other purposes as well: they created the backbone of a library for Rupertsberg, a core desideratum for a Benedictine monastery; many were outlets for her taxonomic urges; and they helped spread both Hildegard's fame and the legitimacy of her divine message. And they were surely catnip for her polymath tendencies.

Scivias

Hildegard labored over *Scivias* for ten years; the name is shorthand for "Scito vias Domini" (Know the Ways of the Lord). The treatise is a substantial volume that would have taken anyone quite some time to write. For Hildegard, though, an added difficulty was that she was writing in Latin. To be taken seriously in the twelfth century, a theological work had to be in Latin, the language of the Church and of all learned inquiry, but not all women had the requisite training to generate a work in Latin on their own. Elisabeth of Schönau, for example, related her visions to her brother in German; he then wrote them down in Latin. But Hildegard insisted on doing her own writing, in Latin, despite having an incomplete mastery of the language. Only then, after she had her draft, did she allow someone else (i.e., Volmar) to make any necessary grammatical corrections.

    Scivias is divided into three lengthy parts, each progressively longer. The first section, which covers the creator and creation, contains six visions. Part 2, on the redeemer and redemption, includes seven visions. Part 3 treats the history of salvation in thirteen visions, using the symbol of a building. A short *protestificatio* functions as a prologue to the treatise.

    Despite the fact that this theological work was prompted by visions and consists of very detailed explications of those visions, manuscript copies from Hildegard's time usually do not depict those visions. The one exception is a manuscript copied at Rupertsberg perhaps around 1165. This gorgeously illuminated manuscript includes thirty-five miniatures (possibly added later), with one for the prologue and at least one for each vision (Visions 2:6, 2:7, 3:1, 3:3, and 3:12 have two miniatures each; 1:4 has three). The miniatures vary considerably in size, ranging from about a quarter of a page to a full page.

    Figure 2 shows the author portrait that opens the prologue (Hildegard and the person who helped get the book finished, Volmar); author portraits were common in visionary and exegetical texts. Figure 4 depicts the opening of the first vision in *Scivias*. To put it mildly, it is an unusual image. Here is the beginning of the accompanying text:

aham pfunditatem expositionis libro,
ut pdixi sentiens. uiribusq; receptis. de
egritudine me erigens uix opus istud
decem annis consummaui; ad finem
pduxi. In diebus autem HELYRICI
moguntini archiepi & Conradi roma,
nouun regis & Cunonis abbatis in
monte beati dysibodi pontificis.'
sub papa Eugenio hę uisiones & uerba
facta sunt. Et dixi & scpsi hęc ñ secundū
adinuentionē cordis mei aut ullius ho.
minis. sed ut ea in cęlestib; uidi.audiui
& pcepi psecreta misteria dī Et iterum
audiui uocem de cęlo michi dicentem.
Clama & & scribe sic.

∫ ncipiunt capitula libri scivias
SIMPLICIS HOMINIS,,
Capitula prime uisionis prime partis.

I. De fortitudine & stabilitate eternitati
regni dei.

ii. d e timore domini.

iii. De his qui paupes spū sunt.

Q uod uirtutes a dō uenientes.timentes dm
& paupes spū custodiunt.

v. Quod agnitioni dī abscondi ñ possunt
studia actuum hominum.

vi. Salemon de eadem re.

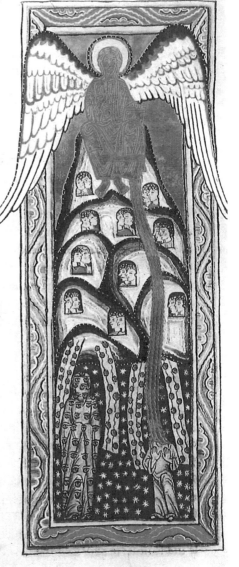

Figure 4. *Scivias*, part 1, vision 1; formerly Wiesbaden, Hessische Landesbibliothek, ms. 1, folio 2r (lost); copyright Abtei St. Hildegard, Rüdesheim-Eibingen.

I saw a great mountain the color of iron, and enthroned on it One of such great glory that it blinded my sight. On each side of him there extended a soft shadow, like a wing of wondrous breadth and length. Before him, at the foot of the mountain, stood an image full of eyes on all sides, in which, because of those eyes, I could discern no human form. In front of this image stood another, a child wearing a tunic of subdued color but white shoes, upon whose head such glory descended from the One enthroned upon that mountain that I could not look at its face. But from the One who sat enthroned upon that mountain many living sparks sprang forth, which flew very sweetly around the images. Also, I perceived in this mountain many little windows, in which appeared human heads, some of subdued colors and some of white.[1]

This image is typical in many ways of the others in *Scivias*, including its half-page size, the extension of the wings (shadows) beyond the frame, the many small repeated components (eyes, stars, circles, dots), the use of size to determine relative significance of the items depicted, the odd subject matter, the copious illumination, the sectional construction, the composite human figure, and the multiple orientations. The tall, narrow frame is a frequent occurrence in the manuscript and obviously calls to mind the tablets that were commonly used for writing and sketching at the time (see fig. 2 for an example). The distinctive style of the miniatures has led one art historian to argue that the brilliant Secessionist painter Gustav Klimt saw and was influenced by the *Scivias* illustrations.[2]

The degree of Hildegard's involvement with the miniatures—and, for that matter, the date they were added to the manuscript—is controversial, with opinions ranging from no involvement whatsoever to the idea that the pictures were based on Hildegard's own sketches with color annotations.[3] An ingenious recent suggestion posits the influence of tapestry on their design.[4] Sadly, we no longer have the original manuscript available for close study, but only black-and-white photos taken in the earlier part of the twentieth century. During World War II the manuscript was taken to Dresden for presumed safekeeping. In retrospect, a worse place could hardly have been chosen, but the manuscript miraculously escaped the firebombing of that city only to disappear during the Russian occupation, taken from storage; perhaps another miracle will lead to its rediscovery.

What we have instead is a full-size meticulously made color copy created by the nuns of the Abtei Sankt Hildegard between 1927 and 1933; all color reproductions come from that copy. Comparison with photographs of the original show that the copy is not exact (as no handmade copy could be), though the relationship is still very close.

Scivias is important in relation to Hildegard's music for numerous reasons. The theological interpretations given therein are those that inform the texts of her songs. The visual descriptions of the Virtues—and the corresponding artwork in the famous manuscript—may have depicted costumes worn in *Ordo virtutum*, as noted above. Most significantly, this massive work ends with a final vision that is an extended tribute to music in many forms (which may in turn have influenced the famous Ghent altar of Hubert and Jan Van Eyck).[5]

This tribute opens with the most spectacular example of musical rejoicing in Hildegard's prose works: an extended celestial concert. Hildegard lays out the texts of fourteen antiphons and responsories (the two most popular genres in plainchant, and in Hildegard's compositions as well; both are used in Matins, the most important daily musical event in a monastic community). The fourteen songs are arranged in seven pairs of an antiphon and a responsory, each pair devoted to a different subject. The pairs are organized in descending order of theological importance in the celestial hierarchy: Mary (*O splendidissima gemma* and *O tu suavissima virga*), angels (*O gloriosissimi lux vivens angeli* and *O vos angeli*), patriarchs and prophets (*O spectabiles viri* and *O vos felices radices*), apostles (*O chohors milicie floris* and *O lucidissima apostolorum turba*), martyrs (*O victoriosissimi triumphatores* and *Vos flores rosarum*), confessors (*O successores* and *O vos imitatores*; this category includes bishops and saints not martyred), and finally virgins (*O pulcre facies* and *O nobilissima viriditas*). Each of these subjects except Mary had already been joined together in the description of vision 4 of part 3.

The song titles—which are simply the opening words of each piece; plainchant did not have titles per se—give some idea right away of Hildegard's sensibility. The introductory exclamation "O" appears in the overwhelming majority of her songs, and the frequent use of the superlative degree ("splendidissima," "suavissima," etc.) provides a taste of the passion present in most of her poems. Almost all the songs in this final vision are substantial in both length and range; they are an impressive musical statement and a fitting match to the expansiveness of *Scivias*.

Although no music is provided for these works (and we would not expect any in the context of a theological treatise), they are introduced not as poems or simply texts, but specifically as songs: "And their song, like the voice of a multitude, making music in harmony praising the ranks of Heaven, had these words" (followed by the two works for Mary).[6] Each pair that follows is again introduced literally as a song: "And again a song resounded," "And again they sang," and so on.[7]

The songs of the celestial hierarchy are followed by two excerpts from *Ordo virtutum* (text only, of course): *O plangens vox* (originally sung by the Virtues after the entrance of the Devil) and *O vivens fons* (first sung by the Virtues before the reappearance of the Devil). These are again introduced as song: "And another song was heard."[8] Next comes a shortened and rearranged version of the *Ordo virtutum* text, again with its components introduced as sounding music: "And another song was heard . . . And again a song was heard . . . And thus the song resounded in harmony."[9]

After the mini-*Ordo* is finished, the vision concludes with seven sections of prose, the first five of which relate directly to music, with four of the headings announcing this fact: "The song is sung in unity and concord"; "The words are the body and the music the spirit" (note the higher role allotted music); "By this song the sluggish soul is aroused to watchfulness"; "The song of rejoicing softens the hard heart and summons the Holy Spirit."[10] The very short penultimate section serves as an introduction to the closing, a lengthy exegesis of the most musical of all psalms, Psalm 150. Hildegard thus saw the most appropriate way to finish her massive first theological tome as being a concert, a musical drama, and an explication of the unity of song, praise, and divine love. Salvation concludes with music.

Correspondence

Hildegard began her correspondence while still at Disibodenberg, with her letter to Bernard of Clairvaux, and continued her epistolary practice almost to the end of her life. In some ways the letters present a problem for modern readers. As previously noted, letters in the Middle Ages served a rather different purpose than they do now. They were quasi-public documents meant to be shared and read aloud; they were a way of making positions and opinions known. Indeed, truly private material would normally have been transmitted orally rather than in writing. Thus, for Hildegard, receiving letters was a public affirmation of her position, and responding to them or initiating them was an excellent and important way of broadcasting her visions and views. They were a valuable tool for self-promotion (which, as always, she viewed as promoting God's will, not her own). She was prolific, too. Almost four hundred of her letters survive, more than those from any other medieval woman and most medieval men.

Hildegard's fame spread quickly, and collections of her letters began being copied perhaps only a few years after she settled in Rupertsberg.[11] The most important gathering came from her late years, when Volmar prepared the most comprehensive and official collection, one of various efforts to pull together Hildegard's works in her old age. Volmar organized the letters not chronologically, as earlier, less complete collections had done, but hierarchically by importance of correspondent. Numerous other changes crept in, including textual revisions that made Hildegard appear in a better light, fresh pairings of letter and response, changes in the names of recipients, and even the wholesale invention of new letters, as we saw with the false "Pope Eugenius" letter supporting Hildegard's writing. While the results reflect what Hildegard wished known late in her life, it is not always easy to identify what was fabricated and what was originally there. Interestingly, one item receiving greater emphasis later on is music. Hildegard's single letter to Pope Anastasius (Letter 8; Anastasius died December 3, 1154) was recopied about two decades later to include the information that Hildegard might "express . . . harmonious melodies in many ways,"[12] a reference to her composing not present in the initial missive.

Hildegard's range of correspondents is extensive: four popes (Eugenius III, Anastasius IV, Hadrian IV, and Alexander III); two cardinals; numerous archbishops, bishops, and priests; abbots, abbesses, priors, prioresses, monks, and nuns of numerous monastic orders; deans, clerics, prelates, canons, provosts, provisors, lay sisters, teachers, a Hospitaller, and her brother Hugo (instructing him to be nice to another brother); and a wide swath of the nobility, including King of the Romans Conrad III, Holy Roman Emperor Frederick Barbarossa, King Henry II of England, Eleanor of Aquitaine, Empress Irene of Greece, two dukes and a duchess, two counts and four countesses, a knight, and the Margravine Richardis von Stade, mother of the nun Richardis. Not all recipients can be identified, and few letters can be dated firmly, but her correspondents extended from England to Jerusalem, and she seems to have engaged in these communications throughout her entire life at Rupertsberg. Sometimes people contacted her and sometimes she took the initiative; almost always, though, she couched her letters as God speaking through her rather than she herself doing the talking. And she was very careful to avoid prophecies beyond the most general. A common query was from an ecclesiastic in a position of authority who wished to be relieved of his or her obligations, to which Hildegard invariably replied that they should stick with it. No shilly-shallying for her!

Physica

Hildegard's scientific work is known overall as *Subtilitatum diversarum naturarum creaturarum* (Subtleties of the Diverse Natures of Created Things), surviving today in two parts rather than a single whole: the *Liber simplicis medicinae* (The Book of Simple Medicine, also known as *Physica* from a 1533 printed edition) and the *Liber compositae medicinae* (The Book of Compound Medicine), or *Cause et cure* (Causes and Cures). None of this was included in the Riesencodex, her quasi-collected works manuscript, which has made some doubt the authenticity of these writings. But they are very likely hers, or mostly so, sharing as they do themes and contents with her other works. And, of course, they are mentioned as hers in the preface to *Liber vite meritorum* as well as the *Acta inquisitionis*. Hildegard may have held back from flaunting these as her creations owing to twelfth-century monastic unease with aspects of medical practice.[13]

Physica is divided into nine books and is a clear example of Hildegard's taxonomic urge. Each book covers one component of the natural world, in the order plants, elements, trees, stones, fish, birds, animals, reptiles, and metals. Discussions of each item, for which Middle High German names are given, do not include physical descriptions but rather whether it is hot or cold, wet or dry. If it has medicinal or healthful value, instructions as to how to prepare and use it are included. Some of these are unlikely to have had much practical utility, such as the directive "If one has the ague, take a mouse and give it a blow so it cannot run away. Before it dies, tie the back of the mouse between the shoulder blades. . . . Let the mouse die between the person's shoulder blades, and that person will be cured."[14]

The section on plants includes 230 items, including a few that are not plants at all: honey, sugar, milk, butter, salt, and vinegar. The 14 elements consist of air, water, and four types of earth (but no fire); the sea; and the rivers Saar, Rhine, Main, Danube, Moselle, Nahe, and Glan. Sixty-three items appear under the heading of trees, some of which can still be found at Disibodenberg today. Some are very familiar (apple, pear, cherry), but others Hildegard could not have known, such as the date palm. The section also includes discussions of smoke and moss. The 26 stones are mostly gemstones, while the section on fish (36 items), though mostly including local varieties, also had creatures for which she would have lacked firsthand knowledge (the whale). The 72 "birds" are mostly true birds (partridge, heron, peacock, swan) but also the honeybee, grasshopper, and other insects. A certain number of the 45 animals are ones she could hardly have encountered (elephant, camel, lion, dromedary, tiger, unicorn), and the same is true of some of the 18 reptiles (dragon and basilisk). The shortest section is the last, which contains the 8 metals gold, silver, lead, tin, copper, brass, iron, and steel.

The book is thus a mixture of the everyday, the exotic, and the fanciful, combining Hildegard's firsthand experience with information she either read or heard about, and keeping with an interest in natural science among contemporary Rhineland abbeys.[15] As a description of Hildegard's world, it was evidently a thorough one. Until the 1920s it was the most authoritative listing of fish in the Rhine River.

Cause et cure

Cause et cure, as it survives today, consists of six books of very different lengths: book 1, 49 chapters; book 2, 285 chapters; book 3, 39 chapters; book 4, 65 chapters; book 5, 32 chapters; and book 6, 38 chapters. The last book is largely devoted to astrological predictions of character—for instance, a woman conceived during the fifth phase of the moon "will have masculine traits, be quarrelsome and spiteful, but also skillful. She will not often, but now and then, be bothered by a light illness. She also can live a rather long time."[16] This section is considered the least likely to be genuine.

The other five books provide more familiar territory for Hildegard. Book 1 lays out the structure of the cosmos, intermingling the physical world (e.g., sun, moon, stars, five planets, rain, snow, dew) with the theological (the creation of the world, the creation of the angels, the fall of Lucifer, etc.). Chapter 22 expounds on a variant of the familiar harmony of the spheres that dates back to ancient times ("When it turns, the firmament makes beautiful music which we, however, do not hear"[17]). Book 2, the longest, peoples the cosmos and discusses myriad aspects of existence (e.g., baldness, menopause, joy and laughter), again with various theological issues sprinkled about (e.g., the devil's hate, the seduction of Eve). Causes of disease are roughly organized from head to feet. Books 3 and 4 offer cures for specific problems such as migraine ("difficult to get rid of . . . entirely"[18]), toothache, hiccups. These cures often share material with the advice found in *Physica*, though the *Cause et cure* versions are typically more complex. Book 5 is largely diagnostic (signs of life, signs in the urine, a daily fever) with some miscellaneous material (the Turkish bath, excessive indulgence in cherries).

Within this pseudo-medical manual we have various disquisitions on humanity and theology, as noted, with some very acute observations as to the human spirit. We also have an unexpectedly frank understanding of certain sexual matters, including the sexual act itself and instructions for an abortifacient;[19] Hildegard is "the first scientific writer to discuss sexuality and gynecology from a female perspective."[20] The presence of these topics led various nineteenth-century writers to eliminate the work from Hildegard's opus on the premise that a cloistered nun would have

44

no knowledge of such doings. More recently *Cause et cure* has been understood as representing the greater frankness (and lesser privacy) of the Middle Ages regarding the most basic components of existence, to say nothing of the presence of widows among Hildegard's nuns. Further, the volume speaks to the standard practice within monastic communities of caring for their own (and very often others) in terms of medicine and healing; infirmaries were expected in Benedictine abbeys. In any event, even if Hildegard had been neither a composer nor a theologian, she would have earned her place in history for her scientific and medical writings. She is quite possibly the first nun ever to write in these fields.

Lingua ignota and Litterae ignotae

Probably the most unexpected of Hildegard's creations are her *Lingua ignota* (Unknown Language) and her *Litterae ignotae* (Unknown Letters), shown in figure 5. The "letters" are a made-up alphabet of twenty-three symbols corresponding to the letters of the Roman alphabet with the exception of *j* (interchangeable with *i* at the time), *v* (interchangeable with *u*), and *w*. The impetus behind the letters appears to have been more intellectual than practical, as only two examples of their use survive, both in headings of correspondence. The "language" is not a language per se but rather a massive word list of more than one thousand nouns, organized by category and, as usual for Hildegard, structured hierarchically, moving from God to the lowly cricket. Hildegard provides both Latin and German glosses for her new words. As with the *Ordo virtutum*, an earlier work provides Hildegard's model. In this case she was inspired by an eleventh-century Latin/German glossary arranged by subject matter known as the *Summarium Heinrici*. Hildegard's linguistic creations may have been completed by 1153 or 1154.[21]

Figure 5. *Litterae ignotae*; Wiesbaden, Hochschul- und Landesbibliothek RheinMain, ms. 2, fol. 464va (the Riesencodex).

The *Lingua ignota* contains numerous words for entities that are also important for Hildegard's music. The celestial hierarchy is an example of this. A favorite concept of Hildegard's, it generated the set of antiphon/responsory pairs whose texts appear in the final vision of *Scivias*, as noted above. In *Lingua ignota*, "angel" is the second word to appear in the whole thousand-word creation (after "God"), and words for "apostle" (no. 13), "confessor" (no. 15), "martyr" (no. 14), "patriarch" (no. 10), "prophet" (no. 11), and "virgin" (no. 16) all appear close to the beginning of the list. No word is provided for Mary, who is first within Hildegard's musical pairs; then again, Christ is excluded from the *Lingua* as well. Hildegard does provide a word for "widow" (no. 17), as well as the self-descriptive "seer" (no. 12).

A single example of the *Lingua ignota*'s use survives, in the song *O orzchis ecclesia*, which uses five invented words. Again, practicality does not seem to have been the issue; rather, the language and letters, themselves reminiscent of the Greek alphabet, provided a mark of learning and erudition for Hildegard and helped shore up the intellectual credentials of her monastery.[22] Interestingly, in Hildegard's second theological treatise, *Liber vite meritorum* (begun after she had created her *Lingua* and *Litterae*), her description of the joys of virgins in heaven includes the statement "And they knew and spoke and understood a foreign language."[23]

Gospel Homilies

The preface to *Liber vite meritorum* refers to "quibusdam aliis expositionibus" (certain other explanations), generally assumed to refer to Hildegard's *Expositiones evangeliorum* (Expositions of the Gospels). These are a series of fifty-eight commentaries on twenty-seven different Gospel readings that cover a portion of the liturgical year: Christmas, Epiphany, the Feast of the Purification, Easter, Ascension Thursday, the Feast of St. John the Baptist, and various other holy days. There is little overlap with Hildegard's songs in terms of liturgical placement, the main exception being the ceremony of church dedication (two homilies, four antiphons).

The Gospel was read not only during Mass but also "after the nocturns on Sunday and other solemnities" in Benedictine practice.[24] The *Expositiones* are structured as phrase-by-phrase commentaries on the Gospel readings, making them homilies rather than sermons. Hildegard is the only medieval woman to have generated a systematic exegesis along these lines. Major themes presented are favorite ones for Hildegard: salvation history and the struggle of the soul to be virtuous, often couched dramatically.

The *Expositiones* fit well with the idea that Hildegard's writings immediately after *Scivias* served many practical needs, just as her liturgical songs did. And just like her songs, the homilies appear to have been written over a period of some time. Obviously enough of them existed to generate the reference in the preface to *Liber vite meritorum*, but others appear to come from later; some may have been presented around 1170 to Disibodenberg; others have references to heretics (burned in Cologne in 1163) and to schism (lasting from 1159 to 1177).[25]

Commentary on the Benedictine Rule

Of uncertain date is Hildegard's commentary on the Rule of St. Benedict. Evidently prompted by a request from a *congregatio Hunniensis*, likely Augustinian canons who also followed components of the Benedictine Rule,[26] the work is one of Hildegard's shorter efforts. It is an extremely practical commentary rather than a theological one. The Benedictine Rule itself has seventy-three chapters; Hildegard remarks on only thirty-five of these. Hers is the only commentary on this document written by a woman, and one of very few from the twelfth century.

Hildegard rarely mentioned specific earlier writers or their writings, but Benedict is an exception for her. She clearly knew his rule well, noting Benedict and/or the rule in *Scivias*, *Liber vite meritorum*, the vita for St. Disibod, and various letters. This venerable monastic rule, stemming from the sixth century, would have governed Rupertsberg as well as Disibodenberg. It is noteworthy for its moderation, and Hildegard's commentary supports that. This is important, for it is one of the ways in which Hildegard is herself distinguished from Jutta. Perhaps it is because Hildegard was ill so frequently and for so long, but she clearly had no appetite for the type of self-mortification of which Jutta was so fond. Instead, there is a sensible emphasis on moderation and balance, evident not just in this commentary but in *Cause et cure* as well. It is certainly a trait very appealing to modern sensibilities, as is the largely vegetarian diet the rule espouses.

Symphonia armonie celestium revelationum

For music lovers, the most important item listed in the preface to *Liber vite meritorum* is Hildegard's *Symphonia armonie celestium revelationum*, the "Symphony of the Harmony of Celestial Revelations." Although this title does not appear on either of the two main collections of her music (one of which is missing its opening), it is widely used now to designate Hildegard's seventy-seven songs, all plainchant. The title fits well with both her description of receiving the chants as yet another divine revelation and with the echoing of her visionary precepts throughout the texts of the songs themselves.

It is not surprising that music would figure prominently in Hildegard's work on arrival at Rupertsberg. Finally she would have found a performing space that she controlled (not that she necessarily thought of it that way), probably with the resonant acoustics that stone provides. Music not only played an important role in her theological worldview; it was also necessary for the daily liturgy. While her nuns could have simply adopted what was used at Disibodenberg—and doubtless they did for most of their service music—anything that Hildegard created after arriving at Rupertsberg would have served to make their ritual unique to them. Both Disibodenberg and Rupertsberg were influenced by the so-called Hirsau reform, and "monastic houses that emulated Hirsau were free to develop their own practices within the framework of a common liturgical tradition."[27] The two manuscript collections of Hildegard's music provide identifications for liturgical genre, making it not particularly difficult to slot most pieces into a specific position in the service. Her musical creations were thus eminently practical.

Exactly when Hildegard began to compose is unknown. In the *Vita* she links the beginning of her musical creation with her catalytic vision of 1141: "Then I also composed and sang chant with melody, to the praise of God and his saints, without being taught by anyone, since I never studied neumes or any chant at all."[28] Her claim of being untutored, of course, is consistent with her persona of uneducated woman being used by God to further his message. To counter that image, her late letter to the prelates of Mainz (Letter 23) appears to refer to the Guidonian hand, a contemporary method of sight-singing that requires at least some musical training.[29]

Whether or not Hildegard actually intended to write a unified musical cycle is unclear, but the idea of a collected set of related compositions is completely in keeping with her penchant for thorough explanation of individual worlds and ideas, as seen in *Physica* and *Cause et cure*, *Lingua ignota*, and the three major theological tomes. And certainly *Symphonia armonie celestium revelationum* as a title fits perfectly with other expressions of her theology. A certain haphazardness in the way individual pieces arose, however, suggests that no overarching plan existed for *Symphonia* proper, but rather that the musical collection developed gradually and changed over the course of the three or more decades during which Hildegard composed. Hildegard's *Symphonia* appears to fall not in the realm of Bach's *Well-Tempered Clavier*, with its clearly planned organizational scheme, but rather that of his Mass in B minor, an entity coming together only by fits and starts.

The *Symphonia* before Hildegard began *Liber vite meritorum* probably included her Kyrie, the *Scivias* songs, *O orzchis ecclesia*, her Ursula songs, some of the Disibod songs, perhaps some of the Rupert songs, and a series of nine Marian compositions whose texts were copied in a letter from before 1153 (Letter 192): *Alleluia O virga mediatrix, Ave Maria o auctrix, Hodie aperuit nobis, O clarissima mater, O quam magnum miraculum, O quam preciosa, O tu illustrata, O viridissima virga,* and *Quia ergo femina*. Thus, more than half of Hildegard's songs probably existed before she began her second major theological tome.

In Hildegard's day, plainchant was overwhelmingly disseminated in collections determined by liturgical function or sometimes genre—hymnal, music for the Divine Office, music for the Mass, music for processions, and so on. Hildegard was well aware of this, as she provides names for common liturgical books in her *Lingua ignota*. Within those collections, music was then most commonly organized by position within the liturgical year, which began with Advent.

Although Hildegard's music was likely intended for use within the liturgy—and perhaps some of it was copied in the liturgical books in use in her convent, all of which are now lost—her *Symphonia* is not structured as a normal liturgical book, as we see in its two surviving manuscripts. These are the aforementioned Riesencodex and the slightly earlier "Dendermonde" manuscript, so called because it is currently owned by the Abbey of Saints Peter and Paul in Dendermonde, Belgium. Collections of music by a single composer are highly unusual (though not unknown) in the Middle Ages, making it doubly impressive that two large compilations of Hildegard's works are extant.

The Dendermonde and Riesencodex manuscripts give the *Symphonia* in two different but related iterations.[30] Each provides the compositions in hierarchical order according to subject. Both celestial and worldly hierarchies were of great importance in the Middle Ages, and we can see concern with hierarchy in the organization of Hildegard's correspondence and the *Lingua ignota*, while she specifically discusses human hierarchy in *Scivias*.[31] A rare example of a contemporary musical collection with an organization similar to that of *Symphonia* is book 3 of Abelard's *Hymnarius Paraclitensis*.[32]

In Dendermonde a single hierarchy is used, while the Riesencodex divides the works into shorter genres (antiphons, responsories, Kyrie) and longer (hymns, sequences, alleluia, symphonies) and then applies the hierarchy to each of those divisions. The reason behind the Riesencodex's separation is unknown, and two items are "misplaced" in that collection. *O Bonifaci*, which has no genre indication but is presumably an antiphon, is with the longer genres rather than with antiphons, and *O Euchari columba*, which is a responsory even though it is lacking a genre indication, is likewise with the longer genres rather than with the other responsories. Surprisingly, Dendermonde and the Riesencodex use slightly different hierarchical arrangements. They are structured as follows:[33]

DENDERMONDE	RIESENCODEX
	Shorter Songs
[missing section]	
God the Father (2 songs)	God the Father, Christ, Sapientia (7 songs)
	Holy Spirit, Caritas (2)
Virgin Mary (12)	Virgin Mary (11)
[missing folio]	
Holy Spirit, Caritas, Trinity (5)	
Angels (2)	Angels (2)
Patriarchs and Prophets (2)	Patriarchs and Prophets (2)
Apostles (2)	Apostles (2)
St. John (2)	St. John (2)
St. Disibod (3)	
Martyrs (2)	Martyrs (2)
Confessors (2)	Confessors (2)
	St. Disibod (4)
St. Rupert (3)	St. Rupert (3)
[missing folio]	
Virgins (3)	Virgins (2)
	St. Ursula (11)
Widows (1)	
Innocents (1)	Innocents (1)
St. Ursula (13)	
Ecclesia (2)	Ecclesia (4)
	Kyrie
	Longer Songs
	Holy Spirit (2)
	Virgin Mary (4)
	Saints:
	Matthias (1)
	Boniface (1)
	Disibod (1)
	Eucharius (2)
	Maximin (1)
	Rupert (1)
	Ursula (2)
	Symphony of Virgins
	Symphony of Widows

Aside from the twofold division of the Riesencodex's songs, the most striking difference between the two collections is the position of works devoted to Mary. In Dendermonde, Mary assumes the position of Christ, between God the Father

HILDEGARD OF BINGEN | *New Creations*

and the Holy Spirit. In the Riesencodex (which was apparently compiled with an eye toward Hildegard's canonization), she is back in the more theologically conservative placement after the Holy Trinity. In Dendermonde, the Marian section begins symbolically with Hildegard's *Ave Maria*—"Hail Mary."

A second change is the treatment of St. Disibod. In Dendermonde he is accorded the rank of apostle (another theological leap), while in the Riesencodex he fills the more expected role of confessor. And the last change is the treatment of Ursula. From her position in Dendermonde after the Holy Innocents, she is moved ahead in the Riesencodex to follow the two songs for virgins.

Dendermonde includes two antiphons not to be found in the Riesencodex: *O frondens virga* (for Mary) and *Laus trinitati* (for the Holy Trinity). Why these were not included in the later, more complete collection is unknown. At the same time, Dendermonde is missing twenty works that show up in the Riesencodex. Eight of these are works for specific saints: Boniface, Maximin, Matthias, Eucharius, Disibod, and Rupert. Dendermonde is also missing two of the church dedication works, the Kyrie, *O virtus sapientie* (for Wisdom/the Trinity), one work for Christ, four for Mary, and three for God the Father. As the Dendermonde manuscript is no longer complete, possibly some of the missing works were originally inscribed on the sections now lost. Curiously, half a dozen of the works absent from Dendermonde fall in the "long" section of the Riesencodex: *O Bonifaci*, *Columba aspexit*, *Mathias sanctus*, *Alleluia O virga mediatrix*, *O Euchari in leta via*, and *O viridissima virga*. Dendermonde has its share of lengthy works (e.g., *O ierusalem*, Hildegard's longest song), but could length still have been a factor in some of these omissions?

Finally, we must remember that Hildegard would not have thought of herself as a composer in any event. This identity is one that only begins to evolve in the last quarter of the fifteenth century; technically it is an anachronism for the twelfth century. We use it because she wrote music, and we, today, describe those who do so as composers. But for Hildegard, music—by her account, revealed to her by God—was yet another way she dispensed the divine message. It was one aspect—albeit an important one—of a holistic creativity that circled again and again around the same messages.

The 1150s

The 1150s were thus a crucial decade for Hildegard, likely beginning with the move to Rupertsberg in 1150 or the year before and followed shortly thereafter by the completion of *Scivias*, the reconsecration of the church, possibly the premiere of *Ordo virtutum*, and the departure of Richardis. New works were soon to come. Passing the age of fifty only seemed to accelerate Hildegard's accomplishments; she would make an excellent patron saint for late bloomers.

The explosion of Hildegard's creativity, which may have generated more than half of her songs as well as *Ordo virtutum*, was made possible by her newfound freedom, even in the face of the monetary and juridical problems that persisted until 1158. Virginia Woolf famously named the two prerequisites for creativity: a room of one's own and an income that permitted the time for production.[34] Hildegard found both of these at Rupertsberg: an entire monastery of her own and, tenuously at first, the financial resources for self-sufficiency.

It is striking how different Hildegard and Rupertsberg were from Jutta and Disibodenberg. Hildegard created not just the tangible works that survive today, but also an atmosphere that was completely different from that of her women under Jutta's leadership. It is telling that in the *Vita* Jutta is barely named, and never in the autobiographical sections. What happened at Rupertsberg is easily viewed as a reaction to the world of Jutta, a world that emphasized self-mortification and retreat from society, with no thought for creative work or its preservation. At Rupertsberg, by contrast, true Benedictine moderation in physical matters was the rule; the convent (and Hildegard) had regular interaction with the physical world, with their neighbors, and even with those much farther away via correspondence; and there was regular production of objects that would outlast their makers' lives.

Further, there was passion and excitement, but it was channeled not into behavior that appears masochistic to us, but rather into a sparkling series of creations that contributed to an extraordinary atmosphere: a musical play; special attire with crowns and jewels and long, flowing hair on feast days; a newly created language; unique musical compositions frequently couched in passionate and soaring lines of dramatic length and range. All of these surely helped to compensate for the initial lack of comfort that the move engendered and to make those who stayed with Hildegard aware of what a special place Rupertsberg was. And although everything was ultimately devoted to thoughts of the afterlife, as is normal for monastic life, there was an appreciation and valuing of the here and now that were unlikely to have been found under Jutta's supervision.

In many respects, then, we can see Hildegard's activities as motivated by a desire to distinguish herself from Jutta and Jutta's legacy. Rupertsberg expressed Hildegard's charismatic personality, one very dissimilar to Jutta's, and the way that Hildegard led her spiritual quest differed enormously from Jutta's path. The older woman achieved no small amount of fame in her short lifetime, but it was based on ephemeral activities such as prayer and fasting. In contrast, Hildegard left a concrete legacy: not just a physical monastery but also her extensive series of creations, copied in multiple manuscripts and sometimes sent to other monasteries. Her fame ultimately surpassed that of Jutta, even in her own lifetime. And now it is her exuberance in artistic matters and her seemingly modern sensibility that endear her to us; she was not a pious recluse bent on self-injury but rather someone with whom we can identify. And it is the activities of the 1150s that established her persona. She could finally express herself fully.

5 | Expansion

Preaching Tours

By 1158 Hildegard had achieved stability for her community. The nuns were economically secure and administratively free from the directives of Disibodenberg. Hildegard had completed a major work of theology, provided a series of homilies and numerous musical compositions for the liturgy, generated studies of the physical world and of health and healing that could benefit her nuns, and invented a "language" and an alphabet that created an aura of mystery and uniqueness for her women. The intellectual foundations were in place for the education and learning necessary for a respectable Benedictine monastery.

With Hildegard's house finally in order, she undertook two new projects. She began her second major theological work, *Liber vite meritorum*, and she turned outward, spreading her message as far as possible beyond the confines of Rupertsberg. She had already done this in part through her correspondence; now, around the age of sixty, she began to preach outside Rupertsberg, ultimately covering hundreds of kilometers in her travels.

It is hard for us to appreciate fully what a huge step this was, especially considering the decades spent earlier in enclosure. At Disibodenberg Hildegard would never have preached; the prohibition against female preachers remained strong throughout the Middle Ages and beyond, and still exists in some realms today (the "stained glass ceiling").[1] More prosaically, travel in the Middle Ages was arduous under the best of circumstances. Hildegard was around sixty when she began traveling and seventy-three when she concluded her final journey; her first trip was undertaken after yet another long illness (according to the *Liber vite meritorum* preface). But neither the fact that women were not supposed to preach, especially in public, nor the hardships of travel deterred her.

Modern biographers have hypothesized four separate preaching "tours," outlined as follows: (1) 1158–1160, along the Main River; (2) 1160, along the Moselle and Saar Rivers in Rhineland Lotharingia, with stops in Trier, Metz, and Krauftal; (3) 1161–1163, along the Rhine and elsewhere, preaching at Cologne, Boppard, Andernach, Siegburg, Werden, and Liège; and (4) 1170–1171, to the Danube in Swabia, visiting Maulbronn, Hirsau, Kirchheim, Zwiefalten, and Hördt. The *Vita* also mentions Würzburg, Bamberg, Disibodenberg, Eberbach, Rothenkirchen, Kitzingen, Hönningen, Marienberg, Elsen, and Winkel as places she preached.[2] It is, however, very difficult to document Hildegard's preaching in detail, and actual dates and places are tricky to line up.[3] If all of the venues listed are indeed places where Hildegard spoke, she preached in both cathedral and monastery; in public and in more restricted spaces; to monks and nuns of numerous orders, not just Benedictine; and to both professed religious and laypersons, evidently with full approval by all authorities for her gender-defying activity.

Trier

One of the most important places that Hildegard visited was the ancient city of Trier. Site of the synod that purportedly provided papal blessing for Hildegard's *Scivias* visions, it was also home to several major ecclesiastical institutions. Hildegard would have known of Trier long before she came to the city herself. In 1138, when the tomb of St. Disibod was opened at Disibodenberg, the abbot of the monastery of St. Maximin was in attendance.[4] The same abbot took refuge at Disibodenberg in 1143 when the archbishop of Trier displaced senior monks from the monastery.[5]

Hildegard corresponded with three of the abbots of the Trier monastery of St. Eucharius, the provost of St. Simeon in Trier, the provost and clerics of St. Peter in Trier, and with an unidentified nun and priest in Trier. The monks of St. Eucharius wrote to Hildegard to tell her how much they liked *Scivias* (Letter 220), while Hildegard promised to send her last work, *Liber divinorum operum*, to Abbot Ludwig of St. Eucharius for correction after she had finished it (Letter 215r; Volmar, who normally corrected her Latin, had died in 1173). Ludwig eventually left St. Eucharius to become abbot of Echternach; one of his monks, Theoderic, was enlisted to finish Hildegard's vita after Gottfried, her first biographer, died. Hildegard visited Trier in person in 1160, where she preached to the public on Pentecost Sunday. The provost and clerics of St. Peter asked for a copy of this sermon, which Hildegard provided in Letter 223r. In addition, the monks of St. Eucharius may have sent her the illustrated "Hildegard-Gebetbuch" (Hildegard Prayer Book) toward the end of her life.[6]

Hildegard created two compositions in honor of the third-century St. Eucharius, first bishop of Trier: the relatively short responsory *O Euchari columba* (nine lines in the Riesencodex) and the much longer sequence *O Euchari in leta via* (twenty-three lines). Despite its short length, the former has the wide range of a thirteenth, and an idiosyncratic sixty-note melisma (six or more pitches for a single syllable of text) in "perFEcisti" that includes two phrases outlining the unexpected interval of a seventh, one falling, the other rising. *O Euchari in leta via*, on the other hand, stays within the narrow (for Hildegard) range of a tenth, and, in keeping with its identity as a sequence, restricts most of its melismas to eight notes or fewer (a single melisma, in the word "Amati," extends to eleven pitches). This is probably the most restrained of all of Hildegard's sequences, a genre that normally called forth some of her most powerful work.

The monastery of St. Eucharius was the burial place of St. Matthias and was eventually renamed after the apostle. Hildegard's so-called hymn *Mathias sanctus* was surely intended for the monks there. Adopting the formal structure of a sequence, it is one of her longest and most widely ranging compositions, covering the span of a fourteenth over the course of thirty-one lines. For its length, it has very few melismas, as befits either a hymn or a sequence, with the longest one (fourteen pitches) appearing in the final "amen." The lengthy text mingles narrative, symbolism, and commentary.

Interestingly, *Mathias sanctus* shares both mode (C with occasional B-flats), melodic motives, and even an identical formal structure with the final piece connected to Trier, the sequence *Columba aspexit*. This work honors St. Maximin, fourth-century bishop of Trier and patron saint of the Trier monastery. One of the most beautiful of all Hildegard's compositions, the work is created on a sensual text filled with rich images and numerous Old Testament references. "A balm exuded from incandescent Maximin,"[7] who is adorned with jacinth and ruby, a swift stag running to a fountain of purest water. He is both mountain and valley, strong and sweet, rising like the smoke of spices to the column of praise. In the recording that did more than any other to foster current appreciation of Hildegard's music, *A Feather on the*

Breath of God by Gothic Voices, director Christopher Page chose this piece to open the disc and truly open the ears of a huge audience to Hildegard's own riches.

None of the Trier works survives anywhere other than the Riesencodex, and they are all possibly later compositions. It seems unlikely that Hildegard would have kept these works to herself and her nuns, though, especially given her decades-long effort to spread God's word as revealed to her through both music and text. Whether they were intended as gifts or generated as the result of requests, these chants surely must have reached those to whom the three saints would have meant the most, whether the recipients embraced these compositions or not.[8]

Frederick Barbarossa

Hildegard received more legal support for Rupertsberg just as she was finishing *Liber vite meritorum*. In 1163 Holy Roman Emperor Frederick Barbarossa provided a charter to Rupertsberg that placed the monastery and its possessions under his protection, confirming their independence from Disibodenberg, their freedom to choose their leader and their provost, and the responsibility of Disibodenberg to provide the necessary priest.[9] This charter is the only contemporary document to refer to Hildegard as "abbess," and she was the one who had asked for the charter.

Hildegard had a mixed relationship with Frederick. She wrote him offering advice soon after he became king (March 4, 1152); the imperial crown was to follow on June 18, 1155. Early on, Frederick invited her to his residence in Ingelheim, not far downriver from Bingen. He later wrote to her "that we now have in hand those things you predicted to us when we invited you to our presence" (Letter 314). And she sought his protection in 1163. But Frederick's prolongation of the papal schism that began in 1159 (when he supported anti-pope Victor IV rather than Alexander III) irked her. After Victor died in 1164, Frederick set up Paschal III as his successor, followed in 1168 by yet one more anti-pope, Calixtus III. Only in 1177 did Frederick reconcile with Alexander III.

Liber vite meritorum

In 1163 Hildegard completed her second major theological treatise, *Liber vite meritorum* (The Book of Life's Merits). This chronicle of vices and virtues continued the interest already manifested in *Ordo virtutum* and doubtless reflected as well Hildegard's greater experience of both in the years since leaving enclosure. *Liber vite meritorum* further bears many similarities with contemporary confessors' manuals with their appropriate penances for various sins. In addition, it is one of the earlier accounts of purgatory's specific components and their theological underpinnings.[10] Although no song texts are included in the treatise, the work honors music at the conclusion (if less overtly than *Scivias*) by making it part of heavenly joys awaiting the blessed.

The treatise consists of six visions and the famous preface, written last, that indicates when she wrote it and what she had worked on before embarking on this latest venture. Each of the six sections concerns a man (who is God/Christ) looking or moving over parts (or the whole) of the Earth, in different directions. The first five visions contrast pairs of vices and their remedial virtues (e.g., gluttony/abstinence, pride/humility, injustice/justice, and so on), moving from the head to the feet of the man under discussion. The final vision compares the four elements to the virtues and then explains what will happen at the end of the world.

Eibingen

Until recently it was believed that enough women were interested in joining Hildegard's community by about 1165 that a daughter house was needed. Rupertsberg had been set up for fifty nuns, two priests, and eight poor, unmarried women.[11] Because Rupertsberg was "full," Hildegard founded a second convent, this one in Eibingen, across the Rhine in the direction of Mainz and easily visible from Bingen. Closer consideration of surviving evidence, however, suggests that Hildegard became spiritual advisor to an existing convent in Eibingen and that she was transformed into the actual founder of this community in the decades after her death.[12] The *Acta inquisitionis* states that the community was set up for thirty women;[13] the house was expanded and renovated centuries later and played an important role in Hildegard's reception.

The Rupert Vita

Hildegard wrote her *Vita Sancti Ruperti* for the eighth-century St. Rupert somewhere between 1162 and 1170 (she mentions Herman, bishop of Hildesheim; those were the years he was bishop). She may have written it in her seventieth year (1167/1168), if a manuscript introduction is correct.[14] In any event, she did not write it in her early years at Rupertsberg, even if the vita serves as an obvious link to her community: "In blessed Rupert there was true holiness . . . for it transferred me and some sisters with me to the resting place of his relics by a great miracle of great visions."[15]

Rupert's vita is much shorter than Hildegard's own, and only about half as long as the one for St. Disibod, as relatively little was known (or, as Hildegard saw it, revealed to her) about this eighth-century saint who died when he was just twenty. Hildegard accordingly gives us much information about his mother, Bertha, a holy woman in her own right who lived for twenty-five years after the death of her son. The *Vita Sancti Ruperti* also goes off on a few theological tangents.

Hildegard wrote four compositions for the patron saint of her abbey (one less than she wrote for St. Disibod). Whether these were created around the same time as the *Vita Sancti Ruperti* is unknown, though given Rupert's connection with the abbey, and the certainty that the nuns would observe his feast day annually, one or more of the songs may come from early on for use in his Office. Each of the four Rupert pieces mentions him by name (only three of the five Disibod works do). The compositions for Rupert consist of three antiphons (*O beatissime Ruperte*, *O felix apparicio*, and *Quia felix puericia*) and one sequence, *O ierusalem*. The titles immediately announce some textual and thematic parallels to the Disibod works: *O felix apparicio* and *O felix anima* (O happy apparition; O happy soul), *Quia felix puericia* and *O beata infantia* (Because a happy childhood; O blessed infancy); *O ierusalem aurea civitas* and *O presul vere civitatis* (O Jerusalem, golden city; O prelate of the true city). However, the contrasts between some of the pieces suggest that Hildegard focused a bit more on the Rupert pieces. Although St. Rupert's antiphon *O felix apparicio* is shorter than Disibod's responsory *O felix anima* (as we would expect from an antiphon), its range is wider, it uses a series of repeated motives, and it ends with an expressive forty-eight-note melisma to paint the word "floruit" (flourished).

More striking, though, is the sequence *O ierusalem*. This is Hildegard's longest work by far, at forty-two lines easily surpassing the next longest work (the hymn *O ignee spiritus*, at thirty-three lines). The text is filled with vivid images: Rupert shining like a gem, the tender flower of the field, the sweet freshness of the fruit.

Some of the language brings to mind the Song of Songs, and two stanzas of the text suggest the dedication hymn *Urbs beata Hierusalem*, which has led to the idea that Hildegard's sequence was composed in time for the initial dedication of her church in 1151.[16] Phrases throughout refer to Jerusalem as a building: "edifice of highest goodness," "windows decorated with topaz and sapphire," "walls flash with living stones," "towers glow red and shine." Jerusalem's "foundation is laid with glowing stones." All of this could well suggest the identification of Jerusalem and Hildegard's new church. The final stanza is especially fitting: "You, o adorned ones and o crowned ones who live in Jerusalem, and you, o Rupert, who is our companion in this dwelling, help us, working and serving in exile."

In some ways the language is a massively expanded version of *O orzchis ecclesia*, one of Hildegard's acknowledged church dedication works, but whether *O ierusalem* came about in connection with the first church dedication of 1151, or the one connected with the final church at Rupertsberg (whose consecration date is unknown), or for some other occasion altogether, it is a spectacular piece that serves to underscore the legitimacy of Hildegard's move and her new abbey.

Explanation of the Athanasian Creed

Hildegard's *Explanatio symboli Sancti Athanasii* (Explanation of the Athanasian Creed) is a short treatise of uncertain date that was transmitted along with her *Vita Sancti Ruperti*, though the connection between the two is unclear. One possibility is that it served as an address for the Feast of St. Rupert, as the Athanasian Creed was normally used at major feasts during the Office of Prime.[17]

Numerous contemporaries also wrote commentaries on the well-known prayer. Hildegard's includes a strong affirmation of the doctrine of the Holy Trinity, something she already explored in *Scivias* (part 2, vision 2, with a famous illumination of a sapphire-blue man representing the three-in-one fact of the Trinity). In both *Scivias* and the *Explanatio*, the Trinity is linked to fire and flame. Interestingly, Hildegard's antiphon to the Trinity, *Laus trinitati*, ignores this connection. Could that explain the antiphon's omission from the Riesencodex, where it is one of only two of her works to be passed over? Did it not meet her current conception of the Trinity?

Exorcism

Around 1169 Hildegard was responsible for an exorcism that contributed to her already considerable fame. She was asked by the abbot of Brauweiler to provide a ritual for a noblewoman from Cologne named Sigewize, who had been possessed by a demon for seven years (Letter 68). The demon supposedly provided the information that the only one who could expel him was none other than Hildegard, sneeringly referred to as "Scrumpilgardis" ("Wrinklegard").

Hildegard obligingly provided an elaborate ritual (Letter 68r), delivered by Volmar. Seven priests, representing Abel, Noah, Abraham, Melchisedech, Jacob, Aaron, and Christ, as well as the seven gifts of the Holy Spirit, were to surround Sigewize. Each priest was to hold a rod. The first priest was given a specific speech to begin the ritual, and at various intervals in the speech (which the other priests joined in) all were supposed to "strike her lightly with their rods" on head, back, breast, navel, reins, knees, and feet.[18] If this didn't work, they were to do it all over again, with the second priest beginning the ritual, then the third, and so on until the demon was expelled. Note that music plays no part in this ceremony.

The procedure worked, but just briefly, after which the demon said he could only be exorcised in Hildegard's presence (Letter 69). Sigewize was accordingly shipped off to Rupertsberg, where, from the Feast of the Purification (February 2) until the Easter Sabbath, nothing worked. Then, supposedly in the presence of three thousand people, Hildegard received a vision that allowed her finally to expel the demon from Sigewize; it left "in a horrible way with a discharge from the woman's private parts."[19]

After this success Sigewize continued to live at Rupertsberg until her death. According to the *Vita* (3:26), Hildegard performed five more quasi-exorcisms, and the *Acta inquisitionis* is crammed with more claims of her exorcisms, though it is not clear whether these exorcisms were posthumous or not.

The Disibod Vita

An autobiographical portion of Hildegard's *Vita* (3:23) tells what happened after the famous exorcism: she first fell ill, for more than forty days and nights (that number, of course, is scripturally symbolic), and then received a vision telling her to "visit certain communities of spiritual people, both of men and of women, and candidly lay before them the words that God would show me,"[20] presumably a reference to her final preaching tour. She then wrote the *Vita Sancti Disibodi* at the request of Helenger, the current abbot of Disibodenberg (Vita 3:25, and Letter 77, ca. 1170).

The vita for the seventh-century St. Disibod is considerably more expansive than that for St. Rupert. Disibod lived much longer than Rupert did, dying at the age of eighty rather than twenty. Further, Disibodenberg was an ongoing community with some records to document its history. And Hildegard had lived there herself for close to forty years. She accordingly moves on to the history of the monastery itself after tracing Disibod's life (bishopric in Ireland, pilgrimage to Germany, establishment of the monastery). The monastery's story is one of cyclical rise and fall, with the fall always being deserved (a clear warning to Disibodenberg's current residents). As with the *Vita Sancti Ruperti*, Hildegard incorporates various theological interpretations along the way.

Of male saints for whom Hildegard composed songs, Disibod received the most, more even than Rupert. Three of these arose in connection with the earlier request of Abbot Cuno: the psalm antiphon *O mirum admirandum*, the responsory *O viriditas digiti dei*, and the spectacular sequence *O presul vere civitatis*.

Hildegard's other two works for Disibod—another antiphon (*O beata infantia*) and another responsory (*O felix anima*)—were perhaps generated by Abbot Helenger's request. But they could also have been written while Hildegard still lived at Disibodenberg. *O beata infantia* is one of Hildegard's shorter works (only five lines in the Riesencodex), with one of the narrowest ranges—a mere ninth. The short text mentions Disibod as "exuding" (a classic Hildegard image) the holiest works like "the sweetest fragrance of balsam," another Hildegard favorite.

O felix anima is similarly limited in its construction. Only one responsory is shorter (*Rex noster*, at eight lines to *O felix anima*'s nine; two other responsories are the same length). Even with this short length, Hildegard is economical in her melodic invention; the first phrase of the doxology is essentially the last phrase of the verse, while the doxology's second phrase is basically the third phrase of the verse. The range is merely a tenth, the smallest range Hildegard uses for any of her responsories, and in fact rarely extends beyond the fifth E–B. The bland text has nothing that specifically recalls Disibod. The work is restrained in many aspects. Thus, these two works might represent some of Hildegard's earlier compositional efforts, and perhaps knowing these helped spur Cuno's request for more information about St. Disibod.

The period of Hildegard's writing her *Vita Sancti Disibodi* may also have led to the composition of her work for St. Boniface (d. 754), *O Bonifaci*. Before his martyrdom, Boniface had been bishop of Germany as well as the first archbishop of Mainz, which was the archbishopric for Rupertsberg and Disibodenberg. Boniface was especially venerated by Benedictines and is credited with establishing the Rule of St. Benedict in Germany in the early eighth century. The connection with Disibod, though, is very specific and is one Hildegard described in the *Vita Sancti Disibodi*: Boniface supervised the translation of Disibod's relics.

6 | After Volmar

Gottfried of Disibodenberg and the
Liber divinorum operum

In 1173 Volmar died. Under any circumstances Hildegard would have grieved; he had served as her provost, confessor, and priest for decades. But he was also the individual who had urged her to pursue her work and had helped make it possible, being her closest collaborator over the years; she called herself an orphan after his death.[1] Indeed, she was never again to work with anyone as satisfactorily. This loss of a close and doubtless beloved friend ushered in the turmoil of the final phase of her life.

Although Disibodenberg was required to provide a replacement, difficulties ensued when they refused to do so. Hildegard complained to the pope (Letter 10), who instructed Wezelin, abbot of St. Andreas in Cologne (and Hildegard's nephew), to take care of the matter (Letter 10r). Eventually the monk Gottfried was sent from Disibodenberg. He was present during the completion of Hildegard's final theological tome, *Liber divinorum operum*, and he began the crucially important *Vita Sanctae Hildegardis*.

Hildegard experienced the initial vision for *Liber divinorum operum* (sometimes inaccurately called *De operacione dei* [On the Activity of God]) just as she was completing *Liber vite meritorum*, in 1163, but it was many years before she could bring it fully to fruition, completing it only around 1174. In the prologue, without naming names, she refers to her two helpers, Volmar and a young woman. Volmar, of course, died before *Liber divinorum operum* was finished, and the book's epilogue credits those who helped her across the finish line: Abbot Ludwig of St. Eucharius in Trier, her nephew Wezelin, and "other wise men." In contrast to Volmar, though, who simply corrected Hildegard's Latin when it was faulty,[2] these later assistants tried to change her style of writing, much to her displeasure.

Liber divinorum operum is Hildegard's longest and most substantial theological treatise. Ten visions in three parts (part 1, four visions; part 2, one vision; part 3, five visions) cover everything from creation to the history of salvation, showing the connection between the microcosm of the human body and soul and the macrocosm of the universe.

The manuscript of *Liber divinorum operum* in the Biblioteca Statale of Lucca, probably copied in connection with the move for Hildegard's canonization in the earlier thirteenth century, contains ten gorgeous full-page illuminations, some of which appear to include images of Rupertsberg.[3] As with the illuminated *Scivias* manuscript, the degree to which the Lucca volume reflects Hildegard's artistic influence remains uncertain.[4] And as with the lost illuminated *Scivias* manuscript, the Lucca codex opens with an author portrait. Figure 6 shows this portrait, part of a larger illumination. The trio is that named by Hildegard in her preface: Hildegard, Volmar, and a young woman. Hildegard holds the standard wax tablets used for preliminary creation while Volmar handles the more permanent parchment.

The Lucca manuscript is different, however, from the illuminated *Scivias* manuscript. The *Scivias* manuscript restricts its author portrait to the very opening, and it stands on its own. In the Lucca manuscript, by contrast, every single illumination (one for each vision) contains an author portrait at the bottom of the depiction of the vision. The opening portrait includes Hildegard's two helpers, as just seen, but all the others are of Hildegard alone. Figure 7 shows the illumination for the fourth vision of part 1, the longest in the entire treatise, which describes symmetries in the world, body, and soul. The year's seasons are charmingly illustrated in the center circle, while Hildegard sits in the lower left corner, again with her tablets.

Hildegard wrote two works in honor of St. John the Evangelist, the antiphon *O speculum columbe* and the responsory *O dulcis electe*. St. John was revered among nuns for his virginity. More specifically for Hildegard herself, he was the inspiration for the *Liber divinorum operum*, where her catalytic vision "taught me and allowed me to expound the words of this Gospel [John's], and everything it

Figure 6. Hildegard, Volmar, and Young Woman, from St. Hildegard of Bingen, *Liber divinorum operum*, part 1, vision 1, detail; Biblioteca Statale di Lucca, ms. 1942 (13th century), fol. 1v, by permission of the Ministero dei Beni delle Attività Culturali e del Turismo, Biblioteca Statale di Lucca.

speaks of."[5] Possibly her two works for John arose during the treatise's lengthy gestation.

Two other works that may have had late origins are the antiphons *Karitas habundat* and *O virtus sapientie*. Each deals with the personification of a virtue—Charity and Wisdom, respectively. These two entities also play a crucial role in *Liber divinorum operum*, and Hildegard's time of intense focus on these

Figure 7. Saint Hildegard of Bingen, *Liber divinorum operum*, part 1, vision 4;
Biblioteca Statale di Lucca, ms. 1942 (13th century), fol. 38r, by permission of the
Ministero dei Beni delle Attività Culturali e del Turismo, Biblioteca Statale di Lucca.

symbolic figures could easily have generated the related musical compositions, although both figures were important to Hildegard earlier, such as Caritas in *Ordo virtutum.*

Vita

Hildegard's *Vita* is a mash-up of material from many different authors put together in the 1170s and 1180s. It is unusual for a saint's vita (though not unique) for having been started while Hildegard was still alive. Hildegard's serious illness of around 1170 may have prompted her to begin writing the story of her life (the first "autohagiography") that would then form a trilogy with the *Vita Sancti Ruperti* and the *Vita Sancti Disibodi* and assist in the move toward canonization.[6] Her material would be used by Volmar, the obvious one to write the actual *Vita.* Volmar's death in 1173 ended that option, and the formal *Vita* was begun instead by Gottfried of Disibodenberg when he joined the Rupertsberg community. The *Vita* was left unfinished at Gottfried's own death in 1176. It languished until the 1180s, when Ludwig, the abbot of St. Eucharius in Trier, and a different Gottfried, abbot of Echternach, asked one of the latter's monks, Theoderic, to finish the work. Theoderic polished it off somewhere between 1181 (when Gottfried became abbot) and 1187 (when Ludwig died), as both are addressed in the *Vita.*

The *Vita* is divided into three books of nine, seventeen, and twenty-seven chapters, respectively. Each book opens with a separate prologue. Book 1 presents Hildegard's biography; the first seven chapters are Gottfried's, but they take her only into the 1150s. Theoderic finished book 1, though not really addressing her biography, and wrote the two remaining books as well as the prologues to all books. In contrast to Gottfried, Theoderic never knew Hildegard and never visited Rupertsberg, so he relied on preexisting material while trying to mold her into his idea of what a female saint should be.[7] Book 2 thus deals with Hildegard's visions and book 3 with her miracles, and each book draws on portions of autobiographical writing by Hildegard. Theoderic also included memories of Hildegard and her miracles written by her nuns, so they were clearly keeping written records of their remarkable leader.[8] Interestingly, an early thirteenth-century abridged version cuts out most of what Gottfried and Theoderic wrote, thus emphasizing Hildegard's own contributions.[9] And late in his life, Guibert of Gembloux, who knew Hildegard personally, added his own emendations concerning her early life to a copy of the *Vita* that he owned.[10] It is to Guibert that we turn now.

Guibert of Gembloux and the Thirty-eight Questions

In 1175 Hildegard was contacted by the monk Guibert of the Benedictine monastery of Gembloux in modern-day Belgium. He is the last major figure of her life, and his fascination with her work generated a correspondence that is very useful for our knowledge of Hildegard. He knew of Hildegard's music; in one of his early letters to her, describing what was being said about her, he writes:

> Moreover, returning to ordinary life from the melody of that internal concert [Hildegard's visions], she frequently takes delight in causing those sweet melodies which she learns and remembers in that spiritual harmony to reverberate with the sound of voices, and, remembering God, she makes a feast day from what she remembers of that spiritual music. Furthermore, she composes hymns in praise of God and in honor of the saints, and has those melodies, far more pleasing than ordinary human music, publicly sung in church. Who has ever heard such things said about any other woman?[11]

Elsewhere he wrote that Hildegard dealt with sleepless nights by singing psalms.[12]

Because of the disorder of Guibert's own community, he spent some time at the Cistercian abbey of Villers in Brabant, an abbey whose location (supposedly) had been indicated to the monks by Bernard of Clairvaux in January 1147. In 1176 Guibert was able to visit Rupertsberg for the first time; on his return trip he stopped to visit his friends at Villers and, at their request, forwarded a list of questions from the monks for Hildegard (Letter 105). She is the only medieval woman known whose theological interpretations were requested by contemporary men, the inverse of the usual relationship of woman student/ male authority.[13]

Hildegard's responses, the *Solutiones triginta octo quaestionum*, form her last theological work, where salvation history again plays an important role. The bulk of the questions—thirty-two—concern scripture, touching on nineteen books of the Bible. Four deal with other theological issues, such as how one contracts original sin. The remaining two questions ask about St. Martin of Tours and St. Nicholas. Questions 21 and 27 touch on music, the former asking about angelic ministry ("the angels resounded with praises [music]") and the latter querying the harmony of the elements ("each element has a sound . . . all resound, joined together as one, like the sound of strings and lyres").[14]

The Nature of Visions

Guibert was enormously curious about Hildegard's works and asked a series of questions in several letters, including "whether it is true, as is commonly said, that you completely forget what you have spoken in a vision once it has been taken down by your amanuensis at your bidding. . . . We also desire to know whether you dictate those visions in Latin, or whether, after you have uttered them in German, someone else translates them into Latin. We wish to know whether you have mastered letters or the Holy Scriptures through study, or whether you have learned through divine anointing alone."[15] He also asked, "Do you, for example, receive your visions in a dream while asleep, or do they come to you in an ecstatic state while awake?" as well as questions about the crowns her nuns wore, the meaning of the title *Scivias*, and whether she had written any other books.[16]

Hildegard replied at length to these questions, and the part of her answer that deals most directly with the quality of her visions deserves to be quoted at length. In the Riesencodex, the entire letter was headed with the title "De modo visionis suae," on the manner of her visions; note how Hildegard indicates that her visions occur with her eyes open, just as depicted in the author portraits of both the illuminated *Scivias* and the Lucca manuscript of *Liber divinorum operum*. The emphasis on light (a symbol for the divine) is also telling, given the many references to light in her songs (*O splendidissima gemma*, *O clarissima mater*, *O tu illustrata*, etc.).

Hildegard writes:

> I am now more than seventy years old. But even in my infancy, before my bones, muscles, and veins had reached their full strength, I was possessed of this visionary gift in my soul, and it abides with me still up to the present day. In these visions my spirit rises, as God wills, to the heights of heaven and into the shifting winds, and it ranges among various peoples, even those very far away. And since I see in such a fashion, my perception of things depends on the shifting of the clouds and other elements of creation. Still, I do not hear these things with bodily ears, nor do I perceive them with the cogitations of my heart or the evidence of my five senses. I see them only in my spirit, with my eyes wide open, and thus I never suffer the defect of ecstasy in these visions. And, fully awake, I continue to see them day and night. Yet my body suffers ceaselessly, and I am racked by such terrible pains that I am brought almost to the point of death. So far, however, God has sustained me.
>
> The light that I see is not local and confined. It is far brighter than a lucent cloud through which the sun shines. And I can discern neither its height nor its length nor its breadth. This light I have named "the shadow of the Living Light," and just as the sun and moon and stars are reflected in water, so too are writings, words, virtues, and deeds of men reflected back to me from it.
>
> Whatever I see or learn in this vision I retain for a long period of time, and store it away in my memory. And my seeing, hearing, and knowing are simultaneous, so that I learn and

know at the same instant. But I have no knowledge of anything I do not see there, because I am unlearned. Thus the things I write are those that I see and hear in my vision, with no words of my own added. And these are expressed in unpolished Latin, for that is the way I hear them in my vision, since I am not taught in the vision to write the way philosophers do. Moreover, the words I see and hear in the vision are not like the words of human speech, but are like a blazing flame and a cloud that moves through clear air. I can by no means grasp the form of this light, any more than I can stare fully into the sun.

And sometimes, though not often, I see another light in that light, and this I have called "the Living Light." But I am even less able to explain how I see this light than I am the other one. Suffice it to say that when I do see it, all my sorrow and pain vanish from my memory and I become more like a young girl than an old woman.

But the constant infirmity I suffer sometimes makes me too weary to communicate the words and visions shown to me, but nevertheless when my spirit sees and tastes them, I am so transformed, as I said before, that I consign all my sorrow and tribulation to oblivion. And my spirit drinks up those things I see and hear in that vision, as from an inexhaustible fountain, which remains ever full.

Moreover, that first light I mentioned, the one called "the shadow of the Living Light," is always present to my spirit. And it has the appearance of the vault of heaven in a bright cloud on a starless night. In this light I see those things I frequently speak of, and from its brightness I hear the responses I give to those who make inquiry of me.[17]

Hildegard's reply to Guibert's question, of which the preceding is merely an excerpt, is her longest discussion of the quality of her visions, but dozens of other references to the nature of her visionary experience occur throughout her writings. She was also quite clear about what she did not see: "I tell you that I do not usually speak about the end life of individuals, nor of their works, nor of the things that lie in store for them, but rather, although I am untaught, I speak and write only those things I am shown by the Holy Spirit in the vision of my spirit" (Letter 161); "I speak more of the salvation of souls than of the daily affairs of people, about which I am frequently silent. For the Holy Spirit does not pour out a revelation to me about the confused lives of sinful people, but only the just judgment" (Letter 339); and "God reveals matters to me about the correction of sins and the salvation of souls, but nothing about how to find treasure" (Letter 358). Various writers have attributed Hildegard's visions to migraine attacks, but if those were the true impetus behind the visions, the attacks are surely unique in generating decades of complex theological insight and outstanding creative work. Interestingly, "an increased incidence [of migraine attacks] at menopause is common," and stress is a trigger as well; those reasons certainly accord with the timing of Hildegard's work on *Scivias* and *Liber vite meritorum* as she begins writing and establishes her community at Rupertsberg.[18]

Villers Abbey and the Dendermonde Manuscript

In 1176, while Guibert was in Villers Abbey, he wrote to Hildegard that "We joy-fully received your book that you sent to us, holy lady" (Letter 108). This book must be the Dendermonde manuscript that contains a good portion of Hildegard's music, though music was not the only thing it included. The volume opens with *Liber vite meritorum* followed by Elisabeth of Schönau's *Liber viarum dei*. Then comes the music section, after which the manuscript finishes with an anonymous dialogue between a priest and the devil that mentions Hildegard and is clearly related to her famous exorcism.[19]

Why Hildegard would have sent her music to Villers Abbey is unclear. Overall, very few manuscripts survive for her music; whether they are the tip of a long-lost iceberg is impossible to determine. Equally impossible to say is how the monks at Villers would have reacted to her music. Villers Abbey was a Cistercian, not Bene-dictine, monastery, and one of the factors most readily distinguishing the two orders was, in fact, music. In their overall zeal for simplicity, Cistercians undertook a reform of contemporary plainchant for their order, with the third stage beginning just one year before Hildegard's manuscript appeared at Villers.[20] Cistercian music theory eschewed wide ranges, ornaments, melismas, and accidentals, all of which are found in abundance in Hildegard's music. In practice, however, Cistercian music does not follow its own theoretical precepts strictly, and even though uniformity came to characterize the order's liturgy far more than those of other monastic communities, it was still in flux in 1176. Hildegard is unlikely to have known anything of Cister-cian musical preferences, and certainly her songs' texts encapsulate her theological interpretations regardless of how the music was received.

Figure 8 shows Villers Abbey as it survives today. Whether or not her music ever sounded there, we know that at least one monastic community other than her own had the potential to experience it for themselves. And whatever opinions the monks of Villers may have had about her music, they remained steadfast in their admiration for her. After her death, theirs was one of a handful of monasteries to observe her feast day (the others being Eberbach, Gembloux, St. Eucharius in Trier, and of course Hildegard's own community).[21] In 1181 they even wrote a hymn in her honor.[22]

The Riesencodex

Guibert ultimately moved to Rupertsberg, at Hildegard's invitation, and remained there until 1180, a year after her death. To modern readers, one of his

Figure 8. Villers Abbey; copyright Michel Godts.

most valuable contributions is a letter he wrote in 1177, his first year at Rupertsberg, to Bovo, a monk of Gembloux.[23] The letter includes extensive biographical
material about Hildegard and a delightful glimpse of life in the abbey. Guibert
tells us that the women "refrain from work on holidays, and sit in composed
silence in the cloister applying themselves to holy reading and to learning the
chant. On ordinary days they . . . apply themselves in well-fitted workshops to
the writing of books, the weaving of robes or other manual crafts."[24] Guibert
eventually began his own vita of Hildegard but never finished it.[25]

It was probably during Guibert's time at Rupertsberg that copying of the
Riesencodex began, in what most believe was an important step in preparing for
Hildegard's canonization. The bulk of the volume was prepared during her lifetime, with some material added after her death. The volume includes (in order)
the three major theological treatises, the letter to the prelates of Mainz (discussed
below), her *Vita*, the letters (this section includes most of her minor theological
works), the homilies on the Gospels, the *Lingua ignota* and *Litterae ignotae*, a letter sent from Villers Abbey after Hildegard's death, and the *Symphonia* and *Ordo
virtutum*. Noticeably absent are the scientific works. The music compositions at
the end are in a separate section that may or may not date from the same time of
production as the rest of the volume.

The dimensions of the manuscript are 490 by 320 mm, it consists of 481 folios, and it weighs a hefty thirty-three pounds. It justly earns its nickname as the "Giant Codex." Physical dimensions aside, though, it stands as a monument to Hildegard's significance as she approached the close of her life.

Interdict

In this last period of her life Hildegard faced one of her greatest challenges. It began innocently enough. In 1178 a man who had previously been excommunicated was buried in the Rupertsberg churchyard. Hildegard believed (correctly) that before his death he had sincerely repented and been absolved of his sins. Authorities in Mainz, however, claimed that the man was still excommunicate at his death and thus not eligible for interment in consecrated ground. Hildegard was ordered to disinter the body. This she did not, though she disguised his burial place so that others could not find it. Angered by Hildegard's disobedience, the Mainz churchmen placed Rupertsberg under an interdict.

Interdicts were very serious matters to a monastic community, which existed primarily to fulfill the *opus dei*, the regular praise of God through the musical liturgy. Under interdict, the musical life of a community essentially ceases, as Mass and the Divine Office are no longer sung. Thus Hildegard—*Hildegard!*—was deprived of the music, some of it her own, that had sustained her for hours on a daily basis over many decades. To any musician—and Hildegard was indeed a musician, even if she would not have seen herself that way—the requirement to cease performing is hardship indeed. It is difficult to imagine a worse punishment for someone who sings.

Not surprisingly, Hildegard did not take this lightly. She obeyed the injunction ("though not without great sorrow," she says[26]), but she began a letter-writing campaign to right this wrong and restore music to her community. The resulting correspondence includes her most famous encomium to the power of music, her letter to the prelates of Mainz (Letter 23), delivered in person. As she protests the injustice of the interdict, she spells out the significance of music in her theological scheme. She writes that "As a result [of following the interdict], my sisters and I have been greatly distressed and saddened," and she is "weighed down by this burden."[27] Local legend has the nuns crossing over to Bingen in order to sing.

She then proceeds to explain the danger of an unearned interdict. The Living Light instructs her about varying kinds of praise, drawing on Psalm 150 and closing with the verse "Let every spirit praise the Lord." She then moves to Adam, who "lost this divine voice through disobedience. For while he was still innocent, before his transgression, his voice blended fully with the voices of the angels in their praise of God . . . but Adam lost that angelic voice which he had in paradise."[28]

Earthly music, however, can dimly recall this divine world. Hildegard tells us that "the holy prophets [an identity attributed to Hildegard herself], inspired by the Spirit which they had received, were called for this purpose . . . to compose songs and canticles (by which the hearts of listeners would be inflamed). . . . In such a way, these holy prophets get beyond the music of this exile and recall to mind that divine melody of praise which Adam, in company with the angels, enjoyed in God before his fall."[29]

Dangers abound, though. As Hildegard explains it, "When the devil, man's great deceiver, learned that man had begun to sing through God's inspiration, and, therefore, was being transformed to bring back the sweetness of the songs of heaven, mankind's homeland, he was so terrified at seeing his clever machinations go to ruin that he was greatly tormented. . . . Thus he never ceases from confounding . . . the sweet beauty of both divine praise and spiritual hymns, eradicating them . . . wherever he can."[30]

The prelates, therefore, must be very careful about imposing an interdict lest they erroneously align themselves with the Devil, "who drove man from celestial harmony and the delights of paradise."[31] Hildegard expands on this celestial harmony: "The canticle of praise, reflecting celestial harmony, is rooted in the Church through the Holy Spirit. The body is the vestment of the spirit, which has a living voice, and so it is proper for the body, in harmony with the soul, to use its voice to sing praises to God. . . . Sometimes a person sighs and groans at the sound of singing, remembering, as it were, the nature of celestial harmony. . . . The soul is symphonic."[32] As Hildegard warns, "Those who . . . impose silence on a church and prohibit the singing of God's praises . . . will lose their place among the chorus of angels."[33] Was that really what the prelates of Mainz wished?

Unlike her fight for Richardis, this was a battle that Hildegard ultimately won. The correctness of her position was finally acknowledged by the archbishop of Mainz in March 1179, after the calling of witnesses and the intervention of Archbishop Philip of Cologne, and music was restored.

September 17

Barely six months after this final victory, Hildegard lay dying. The *Acta inquisitionis* claims that she foretold the day of her passing,[34] September 17, although such prophecy is standard in the narratives of holy ones. The *Vita* poetically describes what happened after she was buried:

In the early dusk on Sunday [September 17 was a Monday in 1179], two arcs of brilliant and varied colour appeared in the sky over the room in which the holy virgin gave up her happy soul to God. They widened to the size of broad highways and reached to the four corners of the earth, one going from north to south, the other from east to west. But at the apex where the two arcs intersected, there emerged a bright light in the form of a full moon. It extended itself widely and seemed to dispel the darkness of night from that dwelling.

Within this light a glowing red cross became visible, at first small, but later increasing to an immense size. And all around it were countless circles of varied colour, in which, one by one, small crosses took shape, likewise glowing red, each with circles around it, though these crosses and circles were noticeably smaller than the first. And when they spread themselves over the sky, their width inclined more to the east, and they seemed to bend toward the earth where the dwelling was in which the holy virgin had passed away, and so cast a brilliant light upon the whole mountain.[35]

The description sounds just like one of Hildegard's own visions, a fitting end to one of the most creative—and musically significant—lives of the entire Middle Ages.

7 | Aftermath

The next part of Hildegard's story is almost as dramatic as her life: how her music came to sound again. The giant expansion of Hildegard's work and influence during her lifetime and after her death—from Disibodenberg to Rupertsberg, then across Germany and ultimately the world—took place most slowly in the realm of music. In terms of the Hildegard revival—or rather, the many Hildegard revivals that have occurred over the centuries—music has been the last holdout, long overshadowed by both her spiritual works and even her medical and scientific writings.

After Hildegard's death, work continued on the *Vita* begun by Gottfried of Disibodenberg. Abbot Ludwig of Echternach, with whom Hildegard had corresponded when he held the same position in the monastery of St. Eucharius in Trier, enlisted his monk Theoderic to complete the book. Since, unlike Gottfried, Theoderic had not known Hildegard personally, his portion of the *Vita* is frequently much more mundane and formulaic than the earlier part. But at least we have a completed *Vita*, and one that ended up including Hildegard's own accounts of portions of her life.

Also written not long after Hildegard's death, quite possibly by Theoderic, were "Eight Readings" for services on her feast day of September 17. Saints' feast days are traditionally observed on the anniversary of their death; aside from the obvious practical reason that these are known far more often than birthdays, they represent the "birth" of the saint into the heavenly realm. The Eight Readings for Hildegard function as a kind of mini-vita, and her musical creation is again noted: "she concocted . . . a song of sweet melody according to the harmony of musical art."[1] A rhymed Office from Cologne, of uncertain date and surviving only in fragmentary form, likely also comes from soon after Hildegard's passing.[2]

Recognition of Hildegard's name and writings got a huge boost early in the thirteenth century.[3] In 1220, after visiting Rupertsberg, the Cistercian monk Gebeno of Eberbach made a collection of selections from Hildegard's writings. This was known as the *Pentachronon* or *Speculum futurorum temporum* (The Mirror of Future Times). The name "Pentachronon" refers to the five future ages of the world that Hildegard envisions at the end of *Liber divinorum operum*.

Because of the complexity of Hildegard's theology, her dense use of symbolic language, and her idiosyncratic use of Latin, not to mention the sheer length of her visionary trilogy, her works were widely recognized as "difficult." Gebeno's *florilegium*, then, provided far readier access to her thought than anything previously available. So popular was his compilation that it survives today in more than one hundred copies, far surpassing the total number of copies of any of her other writings. It was through Gebeno, then, that Hildegard's writings reached their widest medieval audience.

Another key event of the thirteenth century was the official move toward Hildegard's canonization at the request of the Rupertsberg nuns. In 1228 a commission was appointed by Pope Gregory IX to gather evidence for the case, one that had seemed self-evident to those who knew her during her life. Gregory was disposed toward Hildegard as well: "we . . . ought now to exalt her on earth whom the Lord has honoured in heaven, by canonizing her and inscribing her in the catalogue of the saints."[4]

In 1233 the evidence was submitted by three canons of Mainz Cathedral. This document is known as the *Acta inquisitionis* (Acts of Inquisition) and consists of descriptions of various miracles and wonders that Hildegard had wrought. Music forms part of the list of her works: "The community confessed on oath that her writings really were her own, that is the book *Scivias* . . . her chant."[5] The *Acta* was accompanied by the *Vita*, copies of some of Hildegard's writings, and an attestation by William of Auxerre (speaking for all theology masters in Paris) that Hildegard's writing was divinely inspired.[6]

In 1237 (the Vatican moves slowly), Gregory sent the document back, asking for more detail (a fairly common request). Six years later, Pope Innocent IV wrote and asked about the status of the report. The canons revised the report (the marked-up copy was found in the archives of Koblenz in 1882), but whether a fair copy was ever sent off is unknown. By this time Hildegard had evidently stopped working miracles at the request of her community: "monastic life and the divine office were so disrupted by the tumult of people [receiving miracles] that . . . the lord Archbishop . . . came personally to the place and ordered her to stop the signs." St. Bernard supposedly received the same request.[7]

In any event, even had the document been resubmitted, Hildegard might not have been canonized. Canonization had gone from an extremely casual process in the earlier Middle Ages to a formal one by the twelfth century, and in the thirteenth century those recognized as saints were overwhelmingly from the mendicant orders of Franciscans and Dominicans.

The failure of the canonization attempt, though, did not stop the cult of Hildegard. Various thirteenth-century chronicles refer to her as a saint, and in the fourteenth century her name began to appear in martyrologies. In 1316 or 1317 Pope John XXII supposedly instituted further inquiry into her status.[8] A few years later, in 1324, he granted forty days' indulgence (time shaved off the period that a departed soul remained in purgatory) for anyone who observed Hildegard's feast day.

The fifteenth century saw a mini-renaissance of interest in Hildegard, owing to the efforts of the abbot Trithemius of Sponheim. Sponheim, of course, had been the home of Jutta, and possibly the home of Hildegard for a few years before she entered Disibodenberg. The musical fruit of Trithemius's interest was a fresh copy of *Ordo virtutum*. Curiously, the only other post-twelfth-century relic of Hildegard's music comes from shortly thereafter: an early sixteenth-century Swiss copy of her *Alleluia O virga mediatrix*. This Marian alleluia is a work of Hildegard's that fits far more readily into the liturgy than most of her other compositions and was one of very few pieces copied independently from Dendermonde or the Riesencodex in the twelfth century.

The appearance of the printing press in the mid-fifteenth century led to the first published forms of Hildegard's works in the sixteenth: *Scivias* in 1513, *Physica* in 1533, correspondence in 1566. A lengthy lull followed these first editions, not broken until 1761 with the publication of *Liber divinorum operum*. The early sixteenth century also saw the inclusion of Rupertsberg in the famous Isenheim Altarpiece by Matthias Grünewald.[9] The abbey's distinctive profile appears behind the Madonna and child on the right-hand side of the center interior panel. Late in the sixteenth century (1584), Hildegard was listed as saint in the important Roman martyrology of Cesare Baronio.

Meanwhile, the Thirty Years' War took a terrible toll on Hildegard's legacy. Swedish soldiers set fire to Rupertsberg in 1632, forcing the nuns to move to

Eibingen (after staying first in Cologne for four years). The picturesque ruins of Hildegard's home became a favorite theme of drawings, paintings, and engravings for more than two centuries thereafter, especially in the context of the Romantic love for both ruins and the Middle Ages. The gradual disintegration of the monastery's husk, as more and more portions were carried off to be used as building material elsewhere, can be viewed through these images.

By the eighteenth century, Hildegard was generally regarded as a saint, and she was accordingly included in the *Acta sanctorum* in 1755. But the perception of Hildegard's sainthood was not enough to sustain her monastery. The last abbess of Eibingen, Maria Philippina von Guttenberg ("von" denotes a member of the nobility by this time; Hildegard would have approved of this background for an abbess), died in 1804, and a decade later the leaderless nuns, by now only two in number, were exiled from Eibingen, which had been confiscated by the state through its secularization project.[10] The church furnishings and the relics of St. Rupert were purchased by the chapel of St. Rochus in Bingen, which then burned down in 1889.

The pressures on the Catholic Church from the Enlightenment and then the French Revolution made this story of decline and dismissal not unique to the nuns of Eibingen. Yet, ironically, at precisely the same time that monastic communities were folding hither and yon, the concept of medievalism was casting its spell across Europe. Meanwhile, Germany was slowly beginning to find its voice as a nation-in-waiting. The result was that the dissolution of the last monastery associated with Hildegard represented the nadir in her reception, with a rebound of interest already evident not even thirty years later. In 1832 Johann Konrad Dahl published the first book about Hildegard,[11] and a decade later, when the Valhalla Hall of Fame and Honor opened along the Danube, Hildegard was included as one of its charter members. In 1855 volume 197 of J.-P. Migne's massive series *Patrologia Latina* was devoted to a substantial portion of Hildegard's works, and in 1882 most of her remaining works appeared in J. B. Pitra's *Analecta Sanctae Hildegardis Opera*; these are just a few examples of growing interest in the seer. Thus, in fewer than eighty years Hildegard had gone from being the presumed founder of a dissolved monastic community to the object of study and veneration. The seven hundredth anniversary of her death was marked in 1879 by various events and publications.

This renewed interest in Hildegard ultimately led to the recreation of her monastery; the foundation stone was laid in 1900 and the nuns moved in on, appropriately enough, September 17, 1904. Initially a priory, it was raised to the status of an "exempt" abbey in 1908, which meant that the community was under the direct jurisdiction of the Vatican rather than the local bishop.

Resurrecting the monastery on the Rupertsberg site was impossible. The last aboveground remains had been blasted to bits in 1857 to make room for railway tracks; today only a vaulted cellar and five arcades remain, all underground. Nor was the town of Eibingen proper chosen. Rather, the site was a gift from Prince Karl zu Löwenstein-Wertheim-Rosenberg, the property perched high on the slopes above Eibingen. The community remains active today.

If approached today as a medieval pilgrim would have come to Hildegard's community, on foot, the abbey is initially hidden from view on the steep road leading up from Eibingen by the surrounding vineyards that cover almost all Rhineland slopes in this region. It hails into view only toward the end of the trek, a tribute now to Hildegard in its name: the Benediktinerinnenabtei Sankt Hildegard (see fig. 9). The abbey church itself is an oasis of peace, beautifully decorated in its interior by the monks of Beuron in the early twentieth century.

The nuns of the Abtei Sankt Hildegard were not content merely with the refounding of a religious community; they turned their energies to outstanding work on Hildegard's creations, both between the two world wars and afterward. Their major achievements include demonstrating the authenticity of Hildegard's output (previously viewed as suspect by various misogynist writers), preparing a series of scholarly editions of her work, and producing by hand a copy of the illuminated *Scivias* manuscript, the last project of inestimable value given the disappearance of the original during World War II. The nuns of the Abtei Sankt Hildegard, more than anyone else in the twentieth century, have been responsible for the stature that Hildegard holds today.

The twenty-first century finally saw the realization of the canonization efforts begun even before Hildegard's death with her *Vita* and the Riesencodex. On May 10, 2012, Pope Benedict XVI proclaimed Hildegard a saint by "equivalent canonization," papal recognition that an individual has been venerated as a saint since that person's death despite an incomplete canonization process nearer to the saint's lifetime. As much of an honor as that was, a still greater one awaited. On October 7 of the same year, Hildegard was recognized as a Doctor of the Church, a far rarer distinction granted to only thirty-five people and only three other women (Teresa of Avila, Catherine of Siena, and Thérèse of Lisieux, all saints themselves).

In this long climb to international recognition, music played an extremely small part. After the evidently limited circulation of her music during the twelfth century, not a single source for her music is known until the fifteenth-century copy of *Ordo virtutum* and the early sixteenth-century copy of her *Alleluia O virga mediatrix*. How long her songs for St. Disibod or the Trier patron saints might

Figure 9. Abtei Sankt Hildegard; copyright Abtei St.
Hildegard, Rüdesheim-Eibingen.

have been sung in their respective monasteries is unknown; how long even her
own nuns continued to sing her music is unknown. Though often characterized
as "timeless" or "eternal," plainchant is a genre that has changed with great frequency over the many centuries of its existence. A major change in presentation
took place over the course of the twelfth century when the primary notational
scheme for chant, the use of neumes, gave way to what is known as "square notation." In this new iteration, notes are typically square or lozenge-shaped, and in
certain respects are easier to read. If Hildegard's music was ever recopied into the
more modern square notation, we have no evidence of it. And with the shift to
square notation, liturgical culture continued its slow move away from what was
originally an oral tradition of transmission and performance, based on memory,
toward one dependent on notated music. One final change that seems to have

occurred with the move toward square notation is the inability to indicate the many types of ornaments—potentially including microtones—that colored plainchant, especially Hildegard's. Hildegard's music thus may already have become a lost tradition even in the Middle Ages, as musicians' ability to read neumatic notation faded away. In any event, even had performance of Hildegard's music somehow endured in her own communities, it would have stopped with Eibingen's dissolution in the early nineteenth century.

The revival of Hildegard's music began in the mid-nineteenth century, about the same time that plainchant in general—or rather, plainchant as it had been known in the Middle Ages, not the greatly modernized chant then being sung—was itself undergoing a revival, most visibly through the efforts of the monks of the reconstituted abbey of Solesmes in France. The process for Hildegard's music specifically was a slow one.[12] The texts began to be published first (mirroring the process by which Hildegard's music was transmitted in the Middle Ages), and then individual pieces or portions thereof popped up in musical editions of various kinds beginning in 1867. The tendency, though, was for the same works to appear repeatedly, and forty-five years later (1912) only eight compositions were available in modern editions.

The nuns of the Abtei Sankt Hildegard were yet again the ones to change this picture. They published the music of both *Ordo virtutum* and a series of individual songs in the 1920s. While they had transcribed all of Hildegard's music by this time, the worsening political and economic climate, the Second World War, and the slow recovery thereafter prevented the publication of their complete Hildegard edition and critical report until 1969.[13] This remains the most accurate of available editions, though the use of modern chant notation has restricted its popularity somewhat. Not until 1998, yet another Hildegard anniversary, was all of her music available in the more easily read format of stemless noteheads.[14]

Having the music available is one thing; having the performers to bring it to life is another. The process started with Eibingen parish priest Ludwig Schneider, a gung-ho Hildegard enthusiast, in 1857 and continued sporadically into the twentieth century.[15] The real boom in Hildegard performance began only in the last twenty-one years of the twentieth century, however, and a number of factors contributed to making it possible.

The first two had nothing to do with Hildegard specifically. By the 1970s the early music movement had reached a level of prominence previously unknown. This was owing to the growing professionalism of its performers, the appearance of several charismatic ensemble leaders (e.g., David Munrow), an audience that was increasingly educated in music before Bach, and the expansion of the market for long-playing records. Thus, the listening world of classical music lovers was more open to sounds outside the standard repertoire than it had been before.

Second, the feminist movement, its second wave cresting in the 1970s, generated strong and enduring interest in the achievements of contemporary and historical women. As a rare named composer of plainchant, Hildegard was sure to receive increasing attention from growing numbers of curious performers.

In 1982 a young Cologne-based ensemble named Sequentia put on a production of *Ordo virtutum* that was surely the first complete one in modern times. The resultant recording brought Hildegard's music to a far wider audience than their performances alone could have, and Sequentia went on to record all of the composer's works over the next decades. Because Sequentia restricted their repertoire to medieval music, unlike most other early music ensembles, their level of specialization allowed an in-depth knowledge of the music rare for its time.

Despite Sequentia's prominence, another group that approached Hildegard's music early on created the recording that outsold not just all others of her music, but every disc of early music until the anomalous hit *Chant* by the Benedictine monks of the monastery of Santo Domingo de Silos. This best-selling Hildegard record was the deservedly renowned *A Feather on the Breath of God* by Gothic Voices.

The story behind this recording almost sounds like one of Hildegard's interventions. Tim Perry, director of the brand-new label Hyperion, heard a BBC broadcast of Hildegard's music directed by musicologist and performer Christopher Page, and a recording deal was promptly put in place. The disc was taped in a single twelve-hour day, after which Perry remarked to Page, "Well, we have made a nice record, but I doubt if anybody will buy it."[16] After all, who would wish to purchase a disc of music by a medieval nun? But the result was, of course, the now famous Gramophone Award–winning record of 1982, still available today. It remains one of the very few Hildegard recordings found even in increasingly rare brick-and-mortar stores.

Page also published a very good musical edition of most of the works he recorded,[17] and although he never returned to Hildegard, his recording of her music reached more listeners than any other, and, with the edition, played a huge role in bringing her music to greater notice. The trickle of recordings that began even before that of Sequentia's *Ordo virtutum* project turned into a flood in time for the big anniversary of 1998, aided by savvy marketing.[18] This aural largesse created a complex and in many ways contradictory picture of Hildegard's music, for recordings ranged in style of performance from the straightforward versions of the nuns of the Abtei Sankt Hildegard to the fantasia-like renderings of Sequentia to the avant-garde interpretations of Alba to the rock/new age incarnations of Richard Souther. Given that relatively little is known about actual performance practice during the Middle Ages, modern musicians have approached Hildegard as a tabula rasa upon which to inscribe their own visions—a fitting analogy to the manifold visions that inspired Hildegard's songs in the first place.

Hildegard's Music: An Overview

Holistic Music

All of Hildegard's output is holistic; the theology that was the reason for her visionary work infuses all of her creations. Music is no exception here, for the themes of her songs are the same ones that she discusses over and over in her prose works. Sometimes even the same phrases appear in both prose work and musical text. For example, the "balm exuded" from incandescent Maximin in *Columba aspexit* is exuded by Christ in *Scivias*;[1] the "frame of all members" appears in *Liber divinorum operum*, *Cause et cure*, and the sequence *O ignis spiritus para-cliti*;[2] the "sluggish and the straying" are in both the responsory *O vos imitatores* and Hildegard's first letter to Frederick Barbarossa.[3] Even more overlap is found in the use of some of the dramatic characters of *Ordo virtutum* in little scenes enacted in Letters 25r and 58.[4]

Further, music informed Hildegard's life not only through her daily singing of the monastic Divine Office and her own compositions, but also as a source of imagery to be used throughout her prose writings, whether theological, scientific, or epistolary. Indeed, on the evidence of Hildegard's prose works, music rarely seems to be distant from her mind, with literally hundreds of musical images scattered throughout. A few of her references are to a distinctly secular type of music, presumably drawn from her experiences as a young girl before joining the community of Disibodenberg, though perhaps coming as well from encounters after she joined the greater world through Rupertsberg (the *Lingua ignota* contains several words for entertainers, including "minstrel," "acrobat," and "magician"). In *Scivias* (part 3, vision 3), some people are "fooling with instruments used in shows";[5] *Liber vite meritorum* refers to "the pipes and music of impudence";[6] in the sermon she preached in Cologne she criticizes those who are "at one moment . . . knights, the next slaves, the next mere jesting minstrels."[7]

But overwhelmingly her musical references are in a sacred context. Sometimes the references are to instruments: psaltery, harp, organ, lyre (e.g., the writing of Pope Gregory the Great "was infused with the sound of the lyre of the Holy Spirit"[8]), and especially the trumpet, an instrument of obvious biblical importance. The trumpet appears right at the start of *Liber vite meritorum;*[9] the Church "resounds like a trumpet" in *Scivias* part 2, vision 4;[10] God the Father tells Hildegard that he dwells "like a voice in a trumpet that makes its sound through the voice"; many other examples exist as well. Most significantly, Hildegard likens herself to a trumpet: "from time to time I resound a little, like the dim sound of a trumpet from the Living Light."[11]

Heavenly sounds make frequent appearances in Hildegard's writings. Hills and mountains sing an angelic song;[12] the closing vision of part 1 of *Scivias* is devoted to the choirs of angels;[13] celestial harmony, harmony, and symphony all recur regularly. In *Liber vite meritorum,* the Virtues are harmonious;[14] in Letter 348, Christ's resurrection is a symphony; in Letter 140r, Hildegard refers to "the symphony of the Holy Spirit." In Mary, joy resounds "with harp and harmony."[15] In *Scivias,* virgins—the majority of Hildegard's community—worship God as if they are "choirs of angels."[16] In *Liber vite meritorum,* we are told that "God indeed had created man with complete brightness so that he . . . could know the songs of the angels."[17] Further, "man's soul also has harmony in itself and is like a symphony. As a result, many times when a person hears a symphony, he sends forth a lamentation since he remembers that he was sent out of his fatherland [paradise] into exile."[18] Or, put more concisely, "the soul is symphonic."[19]

One musical reference that surfaces multiple times in Hildegard's writings is that of the "new song": "A new song resounded among us";[20] "They continually sing a new song to God";[21] "The whole choir of virgins joins in singing with great desire and harmonizing in the new song."[22] These are just some of many examples. The reference here is to Revelation 14:3, but it is also to the openings of Psalms 95 and 97 (Vulgate) "sing unto the Lord a new song," which was one injunction that Hildegard took literally, to the extent of creating seventy-seven new ones for her community to sing.

Musical analogies and metaphors are the highest forms of praise for Hildegard: teachers "sing righteousness into the hearts of human beings."[23] Music is a reward and a joy. Toward the end of *Liber vite meritorum*, Hildegard describes a heavenly brightness in which "there was every type of delight, every type of music, all the voices of those who sing, all the joys of the happy, and the greatness of all gladness."[24] Some people in the brightness had "voices filled with every kind of music";[25] others held crystalline trumpets with which "they sang songs and praises like those who are in God's presence."[26] The heavenly joys of Confessors, Repentants, Obeying Ones, Teachers and Rulers of Souls, Martyrs, and Virgins all include music.[27]

As already seen, Hildegard's first major creation, *Scivias*, was suffused with music. Unexpectedly, one of her very last, the letter to the prelates of Mainz, was as well. Hildegard's passionate defense of music and her delineation of its theological importance in this letter thus sum up a lifetime of connecting musical life on earth with heavenly paradise. Her works consistently describe a universe that is ordered and harmonious—in keeping with standard medieval understanding of the cosmos—where music is the aural representation of this overarching order.

Dendermonde and Riesencodex

Figures 10 and 11 show the way Hildegard's music looks in the two main manuscripts that contain it, Dendermonde and the Riesencodex, respectively. Both use neumatic notation (the norm for plainchant in the twelfth-century; a neume is a shape that indicates one or more notes). Less common is the use of a four-line staff. The idea of the staff, which provides a convenient method of precise pitch notation in a way not previously possible, arose in Italy in the early eleventh century and then spread throughout Europe. The use of a staff in Hildegard's manuscripts—not the norm in twelfth-century Germany—is a huge gift to us today, for without it we would truly not be able to read her music.

Four lines were standard for the early staff, as most music in the Middle Ages had a limited range that fit easily in that format. Hildegard's music, which typically used ranges in excess of the traditional octave, was accommodated on the four-line staff by the use of both C and F clefs (the latter indicated by a dot and a red staff line) and switching between them in the course of a piece as needed. Ledger lines appear rarely. Although the idea of changing clefs in medias res seems

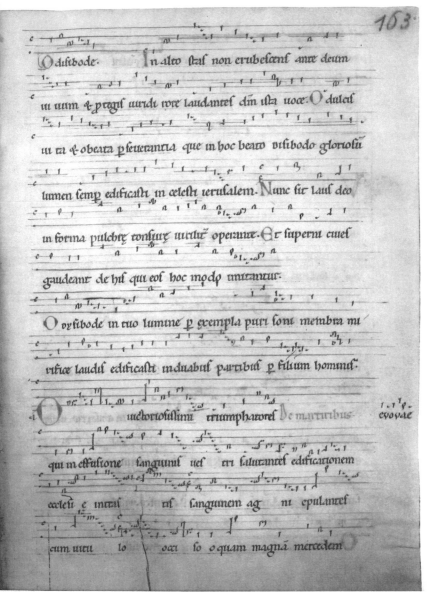

Figure 10. Dendermonde, Sint-Pieter- en Paulusabdij, ms. cod. 9, fol. 163r; conclusion of *O presul vere civitatis* and beginning of *O victoriosissimi triumphatores*; copyright Sint-Pieter- en Paulusabdij (Dendermonde) / Alamire Digital Lab (Leuven).

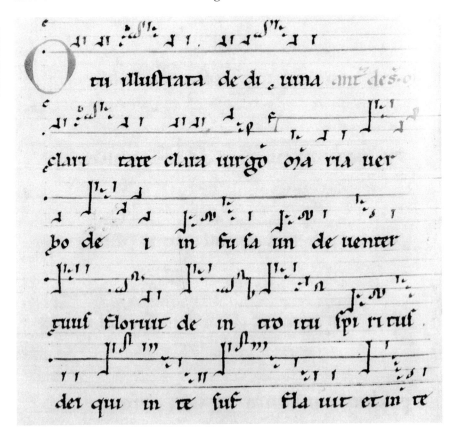

Figure 11. Wiesbaden, Hochschul- und Landesbibliothek RheinMain, ms. 2, fol. 466vb (the Riesencodex); beginning of *O tu illustrata*.

strange to most modern musicians (though cellists, trombonists, and a few others still do this), such switching was standard in notated vocal music for centuries. The two manuscripts provide information for the pieces beyond just the notes and the texts, frequently indicating genre and/or subject matter.

Only two other medieval manuscripts contain Hildegard's music (one has two works and the other has a single piece), but various of her song texts appear among her prose works, as we have already seen in *Scivias*. Unlike the song texts in *Scivias*, though, where each antiphon or responsory is introduced as being "sung," these other text transmissions bunch the songs together, and the texts are not identified as songs. The purpose of these song text gatherings is unknown.

Grouped within these compilations are four texts for which no music survives: *O verbum patris*, *O fili dilectissime*, *O factura dei*, and *O magna res*. These possibly represent lost compositions by Hildegard.[28]

General Stylistic Features

Hildegard's songs fit the broad category of plainchant, which means they are written as single melodic lines. Unaccompanied performance was the norm for plainchant, though many recordings of Hildegard's music incorporate instruments that were known at the time, including harp, psaltery, and vielle (a bowed string instrument). While the precise rhythmic performance of plainchant remains a matter of much controversy and was doubtless dependent upon place and time, the late Middle Ages apparently fostered a practice of approximately equal value for each note. Modern performances treat the rhythm with freedom and flexibility.

Hildegard's music is rather different from norms of earlier plainchant, leading to the question of whether her compositional choices were based on musical ignorance or on deliberate flouting of stylistic standards. The former is highly unlikely, given that, as a Benedictine nun, she was surrounded by music for hours daily through the *opus dei*, the monastic observance of the Divine Office. Further, she follows components of traditional chant style in certain compositions (e.g., structures of some responsories and sequences, her Kyrie).

As for flouting convention, this is the case only when her music is compared to older chant. Held up against the practices of late chant, Hildegard's music looks very much of its time (e.g., wider ranges, modal flexibility).[29] Because later chant has been studied much less than early chant, and also because all service books used by Hildegard's nuns are long gone, the misconception arose that Hildegard was sui generis in her compositional choices. At the same time, despite recognition of shared practices with other late chant, Hildegard's music remains distinctive in its sound. No one has yet uncovered a work that we would confuse with one of Hildegard's. In this she shares a trait with all major composers of later periods: her music is of her time while still presenting her own unique compositional voice.

Hildegard's compositions incorporate a great deal of stylistic variety. A short antiphon using a limited range is superficially very different from a lengthy hymn navigating an extended compass, while a largely syllabic sequence will sound quite distinct from a richly melismatic responsory. In certain basic respects, then, Hildegard follows the expectations for individual genres. At the same time, aspects of melodic structure and modal treatment cross generic boundaries, and text is always an important factor in generating musical structure.[30] What follows is an overview of components of Hildegard's style.

Text and Subject Matter

Both Dendermonde and the Riesencodex identify many works by their theme. The basic subject matter of Hildegard's songs, aside from her Kyrie, is as follows (in descending order of frequency): the Virgin Mary (sixteen songs), St. Ursula (thirteen), God the Father and Son (six), St. Disibod (five), St. Rupert (four), the dedication of a church (four), the Holy Spirit (three), virgins (three), the Holy Trinity (two, including *O virtus sapientie*, whose allegorical female figure represents the Trinity), angels (two), patriarchs and prophets (two), apostles (two), St. John the Evangelist (two), martyrs (two), confessors (two), St. Eucharius (two), St. Matthias, apostle (one), St. Boniface (one), St. Maximin (one), widows (one), Holy Innocents (one), and the allegorical Charity (one), a female figure of varying interpretation. The number of works specifically for women is impressive, with twenty-nine between Mary and Ursula plus the two symphonies for her own nuns, virgins and widows; the allegorical use of two female figures is also noteworthy. The predilection for Mary (sixteen works) and other specific saints (twenty-nine works) matches twelfth-century practice; Mary, especially, was the object of fervent veneration at the time (parallel to the secular idolizing of noble women). Further, additional works (e.g., for martyrs, confessors) could function in general as compositions honoring saints.

With one exception, her Kyrie, Hildegard wrote all of her own song texts, using them to underscore various components of her theology (e.g., the incarnation of God through Mary). As with her prose works, all compositions on her own texts are in Latin, as we would expect for music on sacred themes usually intended for performance in liturgical contexts. A single word in German slips into her songs: the exclamation "wach" in *O ecclesia*.[31] We know that, starting with Volmar, Hildegard had others correct the Latin of her prose works, making it likely that her song texts also had a once-over from those with better Latin.

Early writers on Hildegard generally denigrated the quality of her texts, but more recent readers have recognized their value. Her song texts neither rhyme nor scan, and they lack regular stanzaic patterns. This textual practice is in keeping with what surely provided Hildegard's textual models: the chant of the monastic liturgy. Though not matching the formal description of poetry, her texts are nonetheless intensely poetic and are filled with vivid images, sometimes calling on all five senses.

"Not words but images formed her native idiom," as one writer put it.[32] Many texts employ the superlative for emphasis, and her musical settings frequently reflect sensitivity to the words. And in keeping with her position as a vessel through which her creations pass, she avoids the first-person singular throughout.

Her favorite way to begin a piece is with the dramatic syllable "O"; of her seventy-seven songs, forty-nine begin with this word (fifty if we include her *Alleluia O virga mediatrix*). Even in the *Ordo virtutum*, thirty-eight of the eighty-seven sections commence with "O." Nor does Hildegard restrict her "O" exclamations to the opening of a composition. Numerous works provide an "O" at one or more internal spots, and a few thread "O" throughout a text, such as the sequence *O virga ac diadema*: O branch and diadem . . . O flower . . . O branch . . . O praiseworthy virgin . . . O how great is . . . O praiseworthy Mary . . . O how intensely . . . O dawn . . . O saving lady.

Hildegard's fondness for this exclamation calls to mind a special set of chants known today as the "O Antiphons" or the "Great Antiphons," a series of twelve well-known Magnificat antiphons for the days leading up to Christmas Eve. The earliest of these date back to the eighth century or before; musically they are unlike Hildegard's works. Yet her predilection for the same syllable that introduces these chants, written for a special time of year, is striking.

Hildegard returns frequently to the same images, words, and themes, the last typically also explored in her prose works. Although her texts use direct quotations very rarely, they nonetheless are richly allusive, and performers or listeners familiar with the Bible and the Church Fathers—as her nuns and contemporaries were—would readily recognize Hildegard's references.

A favorite concept is that of "viriditas," an untranslatable word indicating "greenness" and the freshness and life associated with it; Hildegard explores this especially in her antiphon for virgins, *O nobilissima viriditas*. Another is the idea of "sudo" and "sudor," moisture being exuded from an object. Sensory images abound: "unque nos" (anoint us, in *O cruor sanguinis*); "lucet aurora" (shines in the dawn, in *Hodie aperuit*); "concinunt celestia organa" (the instruments of heaven sing, in *O virga ac diadema*); "suavissimum odorem virtutum" (the sweetest fragrance of the virtues, in *O quam magnum miraculum*). Images of building and buildings appear, no surprise given that Hildegard was surely surrounded by actual construction for most of her life, first at Disibodenberg and then at Rupertsberg: "alium turrim . . . elevasti" (you raised another tower, in *O ignee spiritus*).

"Nunc" is used in several telling places, typically at beginnings or endings. It opens one of the church songs, *Nunc gaudeant* (now let . . . the church rejoice);

it appears in the closing section of *Mathias sanctus* ("Nunc ego gaudeat omnis ecclesia," now let the whole church rejoice); and it brings the hymn *Cum vox sanguinis* to a close ("Nunc gaudeant omnis celi," now let all heavens rejoice). It substitutes for "Hodie" when the antiphon *Hodie aperuit* (today a closed gate, with its Christmas reference) was altered to the less specific *Nunc aperuit* (now a closed gate). It appears at the conclusion of two other songs. The last line of *O viridissima virga* reads "Nunc autem laus sit altissimo" (Now, however, praise be to the highest), while the closing sentence of *O Euchari in leta via* commences "Nunc in tua clara voce" (Now in your clear voice). "O quam" (O how) is also a popular locution.[33]

Both alliteration and *annominatio*—joining two etymologically related words—appear, as in the title *O viridissima virga*, the phrase "sudando sudavit" in *Columba aspexit*, and many other examples. Hildegard frequently plays with "virgo" and "virga," virgin and branch (the latter word is used in medical writings of the time for the male sexual organ, but Hildegard herself uses "stirps" for that).[34] That the Virgin Mary is a branch is seen as well in Hildegard's multiple references to Mary as part of the Tree of Jesse (e.g., *O tu suavissima virga*).[35] Another favorite theme is the Mary/Eve dichotomy, explored again and again (*O virga ac diadema*, *O viridissima virga*, etc.)

And just as in her prose works, Hildegard weaves musical references into many song texts. "Celestial harmony" (celestem armoniam) appears in *O virga ac diadema*; St. Rupert "blazes in celestial harmony" (in celesti armonia fulget); the angelic host sings (concinit) in *Quia felix puericia*. Angels likewise sing and "resound in praises" in *Rex noster promptus est*, while the angelic chorus appears in *O ierusalem*. Numerous other examples could be cited.

Despite the many similarities between Hildegard's song texts and her prose works, her songs in general sound a different tone. Hildegard's theological works and her correspondence are often colored with the passion of anger and righteousness. Her songs, in contrast, are typically missing this element, emphasizing instead praise, joy, and the vivid imagery she uses to illuminate her theology. Although the image of blood occurs throughout her Ursula songs, for example, it is the joy of martyrdom rather than the gore that receives the emphasis (e.g., *Cum vox sanguinis*, which ends with the heavens rejoicing amidst images of gold and gems). Hildegard's song texts, so much shorter than any of her theological prose, must cut to the essence of her thought with little opportunity for elaboration. The songs' focus aligns with the philosophy she outlines most clearly in her letter to the prelates of Mainz: music is a remembrance of heavenly paradise.

Models

Unlike most medieval writers, Hildegard almost never acknowledged sources other than the Bible. Although she was clearly familiar with an extremely wide range of literature, the strategy of claiming inspiration that was exclusively divine was a necessary one for acceptance of her as a theologian who was also a woman. Recognition of her various sources has been ongoing in terms of her prose works, and now influences for her songs are slowly becoming known as well. For example, the text of her hymn for the Holy Spirit, *O ignee spiritus*, was inspired by the famous Pentecost hymn *Veni creator spiritus*,[36] while *O beatissime Ruperte* borrows a phrase of its text from the hymn *Pange lingua*. Marian antiphons *Ave regina celorum* and *Alma redemptoris mater* provide inspiration for *O nobilissima viriditas* and part of *Ordo virtutum* (*Ave regina celorum*) and *Ave Maria o auctrix* (*Alma redemptoris mater*).[37] *Alma redemptoris mater* similarly influences *Columba aspexit*, while *O felix anima* begins like Agnus 174.[38] Recognition of such influences, however (and this list is not complete), does not alter our view of Hildegard's creativity or originality, for borrowed material always becomes part of the unique stylistic web that she weaves for each of her texts.

Melody and Melisma

Although Hildegard's songs are hardly uniform in style, as discussion of individual pieces will demonstrate below, certain traits recur frequently. As is standard for plainchant, stepwise motion is common, but Hildegard uses leaps more than is usual, and she is especially fond of leaps of a fifth followed by another upward leap of a fourth, thus outlining the final, fifth, and octave of the mode in use. This is in contrast to much of the earlier chant repertoire, which usually follows an upward fifth leap with motion in the opposite direction. Hildegard's practice is found elsewhere in later German plainchant, however.[39] Sweeping changes of register can also occur in the opposite direction, with scalar descents surpassing an octave.

Other melodic turns include leaps of a fifth in general (especially rising ones, and especially at the beginnings of phrases; twenty-nine songs open this way), descending runs, stepwise rising syllabic lines, melodic sequence, the use of recurring or slightly varied melodic cells (overwhelmingly common), triadic outlines, big leaps, unexpected leaps, and successive leaps—not always of anticipated intervals.

As with much late chant, Hildegard typically centers her melodies on the final and the fifth scale degrees, with a fair amount of melodic circling around these two central pitches. Phrases typically begin or end on the fifth or final and are often structured to explore the fifth rising from the final, the fourth above that, or the fourth below the final. Not surprisingly, the final and the fifth are the focus of most cadences, with the fifth obviously restricted to internal cadences. Cadences can be approached from either above or below, though about two-thirds of final cadences come from above. Final cadences are normally stepwise but occasionally come from a third above: *O mirum admirandum, O beata infantia, O Euchari in leta via, O dulcissime amator, Spiritui sancto*—this last only if the responsory ends with the doxology. The direction of the approach to the final cadence is not determined by the pitch of the final.

Each of Hildegard's pitch centers has certain patterns associated with it that function as melodic scaffolding. The singer who knows one of Hildegard's chants in D, for example, will encounter similar melodic turns in other D chants.[40] Hildegard also makes frequent use of repeated motives or phrases within individual chants, sometimes reproducing them exactly and sometimes providing slight variations. This structural tendency lends a very pleasing sense of unification (sometimes subtle rather than overt) to her melodies.

In terms of text underlay, Hildegard follows general norms for genres, with hymns and sequences more syllabic than responsories or antiphons. In genres that go beyond syllabic text setting, Hildegard makes especially frequent use of melismas, sometimes going to extreme lengths (eighty-one pitches in *O vos angeli*). Although melismas occasionally occur on unimportant words, such as "in" or "de" (in or of), Hildegard also uses them for emphasis of words or concepts that are important within a song ("divinitate," divinity, in *O tu illustrata*). A favorite and very effective place for melismas is the penultimate word or syllable of a song (a fourteen-note melisma for the "ta" of "hereditatis," the last word of *O victoriosissimi triumphatores*). Melismas are also often used for the initial "O" of a work (a nineteen-note run to start *O victoriosissimi*). A composition can thus be framed with the filigree of melisma.

Length

Hildegard's works vary greatly in length, determined in large part by genre (as is formal structure). As the compositions, like all plainchant of the time, are not notated with fixed rhythms or anything approaching the idea of "measures," any statements about length are of course approximate. Yet since all but two of the works are present in the Riesencodex, where they are copied in a uniform hand, general comparisons are still possible (even allowing for the fact that scribes would not copy out repetitions of material in responsories). Thus, antiphons *Deus enim in prima muliere*, *O pastor animarum*, and *Sed diabolus* are a mere three lines (staves) each in the Riesencodex, while at the opposite extreme we find the hymn/sequence *Mathias sanctus* and the sequence *O virga ac diadema* (thirty-one lines each), the hymn *O ignee spiritus* (thirty-three lines), and the sequence *O ierusalem* (an impressive forty-two lines). The eleven longest pieces include all the sequences, three of the hymns (bearing in mind that the "hymn" *Mathias sanctus* follows the formal structure of a sequence), and the symphonia *O dulcissime amator*—thus, except for the oddball symphonia, following generic norms for length. In addition to overall length, many internal phrases are extended as well (and correspondingly difficult to sing in a single breath, such as the final words "numquam lesit" in *O rubor sanguinis*, where the "never" of "numquam" is a bit of word-painting in its seemingly never-ending melisma).

Range

Also variable in Hildegard's music is the range, but here the tendency overall is very much for wider ranges. The lack of actual fixed pitch during Hildegard's time means that her songs could have sounded somewhere other than the notated pitch. It is thus her exploration of what was permissibly and usually notated that is of interest here. Concerning the former, she hews to expectations; concerning the latter, she was a frequent transgressor. She thus clothed her musical eccentricities in the garb of normality.

The standard range for earlier chant is an octave, although Hildegard's time saw greater expansion in this realm. The famous twelfth-century Marian antiphon *Salve regina* and the equally famous eleventh-century Easter sequence *Victimae paschali laudes* each have the range of an eleventh, for example. No one seems to have explored this expansion of range more than Hildegard, though. While *Ordo virtutum* is in general restrained (see the discussion earlier), Hildegard's songs present a cornucopia of possibilities. She has a single work confined to an octave (the antiphon *Studium divinitatis*), six pieces with a ninth, ten compositions using a tenth, twenty-three employing an eleventh, thirteen works spanning a twelfth, fourteen pieces ranging over a thirteenth, five songs of a fourteenth, four compositions using a full two octaves, and one spectacular work, the responsory *O vos angeli*, that explores the huge range of a nineteenth. That range, in fact, was the entirety of pitches ostensibly possible in Hildegard's time, the so-called gamut from the G at the bottom of the bass clef up to the D a ninth above middle C (the E above that D was added to the gamut after her time). Incredible as this range may seem, Hildegard was not the only one to explore it. The anonymous *Alleluia Ora voce pia pro nobis*, also found in south German manuscripts, uses this range as well.[41]

Hildegard's use of the very lowest G is somewhat unusual. The note itself appears to have entered medieval theory only in the tenth century. Although frequent in second-mode graduals (a genre ignored by Hildegard),[42] it was evidently little used elsewhere, with other examples all being late.[43] In Hildegard's music, six compositions use this pitch: *O vos angeli*, as noted, as well as the Ursula antiphon *De patria etiam earum*, the antiphon for angels *O gloriosissimi*, the "symphony of widows" *O pater omnium*, the antiphon for St. John the Evangelist *O speculum columbe*, and the responsory for martyrs *Vos flores rosarum*. Similarly, chant that goes beyond the A above middle C is also uncommon, but Hildegard composed eighteen songs that do just that. Her ranges are thus both wide and extreme.

Exploration of the widest ranges seems to have interested Hildegard early in her compositional career. The fourteen *Scivias* songs, all likely among her earlier pieces, include all five of her works with the widest ranges (*O vos angeli*, *O chohors*, *O gloriosissimi*, *O spectabiles viri*, and *Vos flores rosarum*), and three of the five songs exploring a fourteenth (*O lucidissima*, *O victoriosissimi*, and *O vos felices*). Of the other six *Scivias* songs, three use the range of a thirteenth (*O nobilissima viriditas*, *O successores*, and *O tu suavissima*), one uses a twelfth (*O vos imitatores*), and two an eleventh (*O pulcre facies* and *O splendidissima*). The songs showcase other extremes as well: textual superlatives and lengthy melismas. Hildegard did not hesitate to spread her compositional wings early on.

Despite this seeming profligacy with range, Hildegard actually handles ambitus very carefully. Many compositions begin low and then move high, the progression that is easiest on the voice. Further, the highest notes (and to a lesser extent the lowest notes) of a piece are treated carefully and sparingly. They are often used for word-painting (it is no surprise that Hildegard's two works for angels reach high D and high C, for example), or to emphasize an important text, or to create a climax in the composition. As a further means of emphasis, Hildegard often approaches her highest pitches by leap rather than by step, isolating them through her avoidance of neighboring pitches. Another effective device is to hold one note in reserve and use it only a single time in her composition, close to the end, such as she does for example with the low A that makes its sole appearance in the penultimate syllable of *O Bonifaci*. These choices are all evident to the singer, who becomes highly sensitive to Hildegard's manipulation of ambitus—and all of this suggests that Hildegard herself must have been quite a singer.

Mode and Accidentals

While Hildegard's compositions fit only middling well into traditional medieval modal theory, they match contemporary German compositional practices and theoretical writings.[44] The medieval church modes can be described as scale patterns of whole and half steps different from the major and minor scales that we use today. The four best known are Dorian ("final" on D), Phrygian (final on E), Lydian (final on F), and Mixolydian (final on G). Playing the white notes on the piano from the final to an octave above generates the appropriate modal scale—the correct pattern of whole and half steps. Theorists identified these four modes as "authentic," but also named four sister "plagal" modes that shared these finals but used a different range. The mode ending on D but reaching from the A below to the A above the final was called "Hypodorian," an E mode work from B below to B above was "Hypophrygian," and so on.

Modes were not defined exclusively by scale patterns, though, but also by the type of fifth and fourth used to generate the modal octave. These were placed differently in authentic and plagal modes; further, the fourth A–D in Dorian has the same arrangement of whole steps and half steps as the D–G fourth in Mixolydian. Theoretical exposition of fifths and fourths corresponded with compositional structures that likewise emphasized these areas; Hildegard's works certainly did, and this was normal for later chant. Separation of fifths and fourths also created the possibility for modal mixture within a chant, something she explored as well.

Hildegard's wide ranges guaranteed that most of her works combined both authentic and plagal forms of a mode, and sometimes even went beyond that. Hildegard was not alone in such an expansion; it characterizes a certain amount of late chant and prompts the theoretical names of Protus (for D mode works), Deuterus (E), Tritus (F), and Tetrardus (G). Under these categories we find a grand total of two D-mode works (*O pastor animarum* and *Sed diabolus*), two G-mode works (*O ierusalem* and *O viridissima virga*), and none in F. Thirty-one compositions, though, use E mode, Hildegard's clear favorite and a preferred mode within *Ordo virtutum* as well.

Medieval music theory also recognized the possibility of transposition, where the addition of a B-flat (which would fall on different scale degrees depending on the final of a composition) would generate the transposed equivalent of one of the standard modes. Thus, a work with A as the final but with a B-flat would be the equivalent of E mode (Deuterus); a C final with a B-flat the equivalent of G mode (Tetrardus); and a G final with a B-flat the equivalent of a D mode (Protus). Hildegard uses all of these combinations: fourteen works with A final/B-flat, ten compositions with C final/B-flat, and two pieces with G final/B-flat. *O quam preciosa*, very unusually, has a D final and uses both B and E flats (thus, Deuterus).

Hildegard's works do not qualify as strict transpositions, though, as they are inconsistent in their use of flats. Rather than have a signature flat for B, individual flats are written before some Bs in the music but not others. It is not clear how long an individual flat should be applicable (just for the individual note? through the remainder of a phrase?). Further, the same piece often appears in Dendermonde and the Riesencodex with different placements of the flats, and some of these may even be later additions to the manuscripts. The modern performer or editor thus must make numerous decisions about when and where to apply flats, juggling what appear to be the demands of two modes. While Hildegard's seemingly erratic treatment of accidentals is perhaps unexpected, at least in terms of the most traditional modal theory, neither is it unknown; other examples are found in contemporary chant manuscripts and theoretical writings, especially those from the Rhineland.[45] Southern Germany evidently enjoyed much greater freedom in modal orientation than other parts of Europe.

Other compositions match neither the standard modes nor strictly transposed ones. Although Hildegard's choices in these compositions are not common, they are also not unique for the late Middle Ages. The finals A, B, and C (and no accidentals) are each found in a single work: *O beata infantia*, *O viriditas digiti dei*, and *Vos flores rosarum*, respectively. Nine works have a D final and sporadic use of a B-flat. The Kyrie has an F final and a B-flat (this last combination became increasingly frequent in the Middle Ages and beyond, as musicians viewed the F–B tritone as "the devil in music"). And two works, *O vos angeli* and *Studium divinitatis*, share the rare combination of E final and use of B-flat. A good half of Hildegard's works, then, use some kind of mixed mode, and that percentage is far higher if we include pieces that combine authentic and plagal forms of a mode.

Three of Hildegard's compositions begin somewhere other than the final of the piece's mode, a practice found in other plainchant besides hers. In *O virgo ecclesia*, an E-mode work, the first pitch is F, and the melody meanders briefly before reaching the pitch E at the end of "O." This off-kilter start was perhaps used to set the mood for the work's subject of an implied ecclesiastical revolt.

A second work, *O tu illustrata*, has a D final and use of B-flat. The work begins on G, but the G functions as lower neighbor to A, the fifth scale degree, and is part of a masterly trifold repetition that delays resolution to the anticipated D until the symbolic word "Maria" is reached. In this piece, to be discussed in detail later, Hildegard plays brilliantly with aural expectations.

A third composition is more unusual. *O lucidissima* truly begins in one tonal center and ends in another, moving from F (with flat) to G (also with flat). The last cadence on F is for the word "opening"; the tonal shift that follows begins appropriately with the words "the enclosure of the power of the devil." And although a textual function accompanies the shift, a musical reason underlies it as well. For the opening of the piece, Hildegard has transformed her Kyrie into a less predictable melodic line for "O brightest multitude of Apostles, rising in true knowledge."

9 | Liturgy and Shorter Genres

Liturgy

The two main components of the monastic liturgy, the Mass and the Divine Office, were governed by two continuous and simultaneous cycles of the church year. The Temporale (Cycle of the Time), which took precedence, celebrated Christ's teachings and marked the events of his life on Earth and his death, resurrection, and ascension. It contained both fixed feasts (of unchanging date, such as Christmas) and movable feasts (the vast majority, such as Easter), whose dates varied from year to year. Most, though not all, Temporale feasts took place on Sundays throughout the year.

The Sanctorale (Cycle of the Saints) was, by contrast, entirely composed of fixed feasts. Every day of the year marked the feast of one or more saints, including the key events of Mary's life. Some Sanctorale feasts were universal (St. John the Baptist on June 24, for example), while others were celebrated only locally (e.g., saints such as Rupert and Disibod).

Chant for both the Temporale and Sanctorale fell into two musical types: liturgical recitative and composed chant. Liturgical recitative consisted of formulas of repeated notes with small gestures to mark beginnings, ends, and significant internal points. The formulas could be expanded or contracted as needed to fit the amount of text to be recited, so they provided a kind of "one size fits all" template for many different texts. The relative lack of musical interest focused attention on the text, and liturgical recitative was thus used for the many readings within a service (e.g., Gospel, Epistle, psalms). Composed chant, in contrast, fit a specific melody to a specific text. Text remained important, but the musical expression of the text was also important. Readings in (musically subdued) liturgical recitative were typically followed by the musically powerful reactions of composed chant. All of Hildegard's works are composed chant, including, as we shall see, texts that were more frequently sung to liturgical recitative.

The Mass and Divine Office each day would include two types of texts: those whose words were unchanging, called Ordinary texts (e.g., Kyrie), and those whose words varied according to the Temporale or Sanctorale feast being celebrated, called Proper texts (e.g., responsory texts). Medieval composers concentrated on setting Proper texts, and Hildegard was no exception: she composed music for only one Ordinary text, that of the Kyrie for the Mass. Hildegard likewise emphasized texts that were used in the Divine Office; her music that could be used in the Mass consists only of her Kyrie, a single alleluia, and seven sequences.

The medieval Divine Office consisted of eight services, sung daily. They extended across most of an individual day, from Matins (in the wee hours of the morning), through Lauds and Prime (at the beginning of the day), to Terce, Sext, and None (at regular intervals throughout the daytime), and finally concluding with Vespers and Compline at the end of the day. Matins was the longest and most complex, with Vespers and Lauds next in weight. The others, the "little hours," were relatively short, since they were interruptions in the *opus mundi* of the workday. Celebration of the most important feast days began with Vespers on the eve of the feast and extended through the eight services of the feast day itself. Thus, big feasts would have both First Vespers (on the eve of the feast) and Second Vespers (on the feast day).

As Benedictine nuns, Hildegard and her community were required to perform the daily Divine Office as well as celebrate Mass. All of this was sung throughout; these are the standard sites for music in monastic surroundings. In Letter 296r (to "O., the Priest"), Hildegard uses the Offices Prime, Terce, Sext, and None as analogies for stages in life, confirming her knowledge of the monastic ritual (if any confirmation were needed); in the crucially significant letter to the prelates of Mainz, she documents her following the requirements of the interdict by saying, "We have . . . ceased from singing the divine praises and from participation in the Mass. . . . We have ceased to sing the divine office, merely reading it instead."[1] The *Lingua ignota*, meanwhile, contains numerous words connected with the Divine

Service, beginning with a series of liturgical books: missal (a book combining chants, prayers, and readings for the Mass), lectionary (containing the lessons to be read at Mass), evangeliary (lessons from the Gospels), gradual (containing the Proper chants of the Mass), antiphoner (containing chants for the Divine Office), hymnal, collectar (containing the collects and often other material used in the Office), psalter, homiliary (excerpts from the Church Fathers to be read at Matins), breviary (chants, prayers, and lessons for the Divine Office), "Matins book," and the unexplained "cursere." The *Lingua* contains as well names of specific liturgical components—antiphon, responsory, verse, psalm, collect, and chapter—along with six of the Offices (Prime, Terce, Sext, None, Vespers, and Compline). Life at Rupertsberg was accompanied by the constant sound of music.

Placement in the Liturgical Year

Because the manuscripts of Hildegard's music are organized by theme, in contrast to more normal medieval music manuscripts that are structured by the Temporale and Sanctorale, determining the precise liturgical placement of Hildegard's pieces presents one more problem connected with her music.

Songs for specific saints would have been performed on their appropriate feast days and eves and other relevant feasts, such as the translation of relics or the octave of a feast (one week after the feast itself). Over the course of the year, these days would have been February 24 for St. Matthias, apostle; May 15 for St. Rupert; May 29 for St. Maximin; June 5 for St. Boniface; October 21 for St. Ursula and the 11,000 Virgins; December 8 for St. Eucharius; and December 27 for St. John the Evangelist. Both July 8 and September 8 are cited for St. Disibod; in her vita for the saint, Hildegard says he died on the eighth day of the Ides of June, thus June 20. His relics were translated on November 1, 1139.[2]

Other dates in the liturgical calendar fit with additional compositions. December 28, the Feast of the Holy Innocents, was surely the date that Hildegard's responsory for that group, *Rex noster promptus est*, was performed. September 29, the Feast of St. Michael the Archangel, may have worked for the two songs for angels. Pentecost Sunday would have been an appropriate place for the three works for the Holy Spirit. If *Karitas habundat* refers to the Holy Spirit, as some suggest (it follows *Spiritus sanctus vivificans vita* in both manuscripts), this antiphon would also work on Pentecost. The following Sunday, Trinity Sunday, is perhaps the likeliest day for the antiphon *Laus trinitati*. That feast would also work well for the antiphon *O virtus sapientie*. Though the work addresses the virtue Wisdom, that figure's three wings are described in terms that mark them as clear allegories for the three components of the Trinity.

Two works conclude with an "alleluia" added at the end, an acclamation appended to chants during Paschaltide. One of these, *Nunc gaudeant*, has already been mentioned as possibly coming from just that period in 1155. The other, *O beatissime Ruperte*, would suit the Feast of St. Rupert on May 15, a date that falls within Paschaltide whenever Easter falls on March 27 or later (thus, most years).

A piece needing no specific date is, of course, the Kyrie, which would fit into any Mass as well as other places in the liturgy. Almost as flexible are the many works for Mary (sixteen, more than for any other individual). The numerous Marian feasts celebrated throughout the year provided ample opportunity for compositions celebrating Mary, and votive rituals in her honor were the most common throughout the Middle Ages and beyond. And, of course, we know that Hildegard herself roamed the halls singing the Marian sequence *O virga ac diadema*.

Once past the Marian works it becomes somewhat more difficult to determine appropriate moments for performance of the remaining pieces. The Temporale, for example, observes the life of Christ and his preaching, but Hildegard's chants for God do not fit neatly into Temporale feasts. The responsory *O vis eternitatis* celebrates both Father and Son and is thus general rather than specific. The poetic imagery of *O cruor sanguinis* refers to the sacrifice of Christ but is more specifically a request for his aid against weakness—thus, another fairly generic function.

The antiphons *O eterne deus* and *O magne pater* are both prayers directed to God the Father. Indeed, both refer to need: "we are in great need" (in magna necessitate sumus) in *O magne pater*; "look upon this need" (inspice necessitatem hanc) in *O eterne deus*. Antiphons *O pastor animarum* and *O quam mirabilis* are also specifically for God the Father, and *O pastor animarum* once more includes a request for help: "free us from our miseries and our weaknesses" (nos liberare de miseriis et languoribus nostris). Perhaps the works requesting aid were generated by a crisis faced by Hildegard and her nuns (there were many, after all) and used in a votive Mass or service. Bland as these requests may seem, they are relatively rare in Hildegard's output; her songs far more often sing the praises of those she is celebrating.

Also not rigidly fixed in the standard round of the liturgical year are the antiphon/responsory pairs for the celestial hierarchy. Works for Mary in the celestial hierarchy, as noted, could fit into the numerous Marian feasts or votive services. The liturgy also provides for observances for apostles, martyrs, confessors, and virgins (the "Common of the Saints") for those saints not indicated by name in the Sanctorale, thus providing a site for those components of Hildegard's hierarchy. Aside from these general celebrations, all of these categories but confessors also formed part of the observance of All Saints' Day on November 1.[3] Interestingly, during Hildegard's time at Disibodenberg, altars were dedicated to Mary, martyrs, confessors, and so on—all members of the celestial hierarchy she honors in her music.[4]

The church dedication antiphons, obviously, would be sung when a church was first dedicated, but they would also be sung on anniversaries of the dedication. Only the "symphony of virgins" and "symphony of widows" are thus unaccounted for in terms of performance possibilities. The former could fit into feasts celebrating a virgin or virgins, but the uniqueness of the symphony as a genre suggests performance out of the ordinary. Perhaps the two symphonies were composed for and performed at the ceremonies when a new member of Rupertsberg took her final vows.

Genre

Almost all of Hildegard's compositions are identified by liturgical genre in one or both main music manuscripts (Dendermonde and the Riesencodex; a single piece, the responsory *O vos felices radices*, is mislabeled in Dendermonde). The works usually follow the basic generic standards of the time, although occasionally regular formal structures are jettisoned in favor of through-composition. Further, most of the genres employed fit readily into the standard liturgy. Thus, the simplest answer to the question of how the music was used—that Hildegard wrote most of her songs for performance by her nuns within the liturgy— appears to be the likeliest one. Some of the pieces may have been used as well for processions or devotional services, and as noted, the two symphoniae do not fit into any standard liturgical position.

Hildegard's seventy-eight compositions are categorized as follows: forty-three antiphons, eighteen responsories, seven sequences, four hymns, two symphoniae, one Kyrie, one alleluia, and one work assigned to no genre (thus, seventy-seven individual songs), plus one musical drama. As we will see, not all pieces within those categories adhere to generic norms. Hildegard's preference for antiphons and responsories mirrors the overall distribution of the plainchant repertory, where those two genres outnumber all others. Appropriately enough, the *Lingua ignota* includes words for both antiphon and responsory as well as a word for "verse," a subdivision of a responsory.

By Hildegard's day, a complete liturgy had long been available to the monastic community, which meant that not all genres or subjects received equal compositional attention. Saints' Offices were the focus of much work, and music for the ever expanding cult of Mary remained in demand. Within the Mass, Ordinary chants (with the exception of the Credo) were still being written in the twelfth century, though most often with troped texts. By contrast, chants for the Mass Proper were essentially in place by the ninth century, with the exception of alleluias and the new genre of sequence. Hildegard's choices for Mass composition, then—one Kyrie, one alleluia, and seven sequences—are in keeping with twelfth-century preferences, as is her emphasis on music for the Divine Office.

Kyrie

The Kyrie is an unusual work for Hildegard in many ways. It is the only work for which she did not write the text. It is the shortest text that she sets. It is the only text not in Latin; it is Greek. It is her only work with an F final. It is her only work using repetition to such a great extent. It is the only composition that she subsumes into another work. It is her only setting of a Mass Ordinary text (a text that is used in the Mass no matter what feast is being celebrated). Hildegard's Kyrie shares some melodic material with a twelfth-century German Kyrie as well as an anonymous one transmitted in German and other sources,[5] all considerably after Hildegard's death.[6] This shared material again places Hildegard within contemporary musical traditions.

Hildegard's Kyrie follows a structure frequently used in other works of this genre. All Kyries have a standard ninefold textual layout: "Kyrie eleison" (Lord have mercy) three times, "Christe eleison" (Christ have mercy) three times, "Kyrie eleison" three times. Hildegard's work provides music for the initial Kyrie with one phrase for "Kyrie" (a) and another for "eleison" (b). The initial section, written out once in the music, would then have been sung twice more. New music—albeit borrowing a few motives from the Kyrie—appears for the Christe, which again would have been sung twice more. The return to the Kyrie text brings a new phrase for "Kyrie," while the "eleison" brings back a very slightly varied version of the "b" motive used for the first Kyrie. This whole phrase (the "Kyrie" music and the "eleison" music) would have been repeated, even though it is written only once. The final "Kyrie eleison," completely written out, begins as a literal repeat of the preceding "Kyrie eleison" but provides a varied ending. This tightly interwoven piece thus looks like the following:

Kyrie	a
eleison	b
[Kyrie eleison]	
[Kyrie eleison]	
Christe eleison	c (with motives from b)
[Christe eleison]	
[Christe eleison]	
Kyrie	d
eleison	b'
[Kyrie eleison]	
Kyrie	d
eleison	b"

The short text provides opportunities for melismatic writing, one of Hildegard's favorite practices and common for Kyries; the same is true for the sharing of motives and melodic shapes among sections.

As mentioned, the Kyrie is unusual as well in forming part of another of her compositions; in a smudged version, it provides the opening of the responsory for apostles, *O lucidissima*. The fact that *O lucidissima* almost ignores the usual formal plan of a responsory is further suggestive of a cobbled-together genesis for the piece.

The many ways in which the Kyrie is unusual in Hildegard's output has led some to think it is not by her and that it was composed (extracted, that is, from *O lucidissima*) to serve as a filler composition between the "short genres" section of the Riesencodex and the "long genres" section (it does not appear in Dendermonde). That is the most obvious place for it under any circumstances, as it does not fit into the hierarchical scheme of the manuscript. And from the point of view of compositional process, it is far likelier that a carefully constructed and balanced work (the Kyrie) was then altered to form the opening of the sole Hildegard composition (*O lucidissima*) that begins firmly in one modal universe and ends in another rather than having such a symmetrical piece generated from its more freewheeling treatment. Hildegard's Kyrie further shares various traits of late Kyries (Kyrie composition was ongoing in the twelfth century and even later, though more often with troped texts), including scale passages, broken "chords," the use of F with B-flat, and exploration of the upper octave.

What is far likelier than the "not by Hildegard" scenario is that it was her very first compositional effort, using the simplest of liturgical texts and following a clear-cut layout and straightforward modal plan—testing the waters before embarking on complexities such as those of the early *Scivias* songs. Indeed, as the most public of any of Hildegard's works, the Kyrie is a highly appropriate place for this most conservative approach. As noted earlier, the work could have been sung in daily Mass, was part of three of the daily Offices, and formed a component of the ceremony for the dedication of churches.

Antiphon

Hildegard's forty-three antiphons are her most numerous and in many ways her most diverse set of pieces, ranging from very short works (i.e., three staves each in the Riesencodex for *O pastor animarum*, *Deus enim in prima*, and *Sed diabolus*) to the far more substantial *O tu illustrata* (seventeen staves in the Riesencodex), from her only work of a mere octave (*Studium divinitatis*) to three works of a full two octaves in range (*O chohors milicie floris*, *O gloriosissimi*, and *O spectabiles viri*; these three works are exceeded in range only by the responsory *O vos angeli*). One short work, *O cruor sanguinis*, was left incomplete in its sole source, the Riesencodex, with the full text written out but music filled in for only three of its four staves. More than half (twenty-six) of Hildegard's forty-nine "O" compositions are antiphons, which is fitting given that the use of an initial "O" calls to mind the traditional "O Antiphons" of Advent.

The prominent position that antiphons hold in Hildegard's output matches their position in the chant repertory overall, where they are the dominant genre. Several types of antiphons exist, but the most frequent is the "psalm antiphon," an antiphon that both precedes and follows the singing of a psalm or psalm verse. Psalms were sung in each component of the Divine Office, and psalm verses were used in the introit of the Mass, but the most elaborate of their accompanying antiphons appeared in the three major Offices: Matins, Lauds, and Vespers.

Because psalms are from the Old Testament, and thus contain no reference to Christ, psalms were "Christianized" in performance by the addition of the Lesser Doxology: Glory be to the Father, and to the Son, and to the Holy Spirit, as it was in the beginning, is now, and ever shall be, world without end, amen. The basic performance structure was thus antiphon / psalm (or psalm verse) / Lesser Doxology / repeat of the antiphon. Both the psalm and the Lesser Doxology were sung to largely syllabic melodic formulas whose repetitive phrases contrasted with the composed melodies of the antiphon. The formulas for the psalm and doxology recitation were typically memorized rather than written out, with the exception of the conclusion of the doxology. Because the doxology had to lead back to the repeat of the antiphon, the pitches for its closing were indicated along with the vowels E–U–O–U–A–E—the vowels for the closing words "seculorum amen." This unit was known as a *differentia*.

Antiphons were also used to frame the Office canticles, of which the most important were those in Lauds and Vespers. A canticle is a lyrical biblical text from somewhere other than the Psalms; it was sung to recitational chant. In Lauds the text is the Benedictus, the Song of Zachariah (Luke 1:68–79) and in Vespers it is the Magnificat, the Song of the Virgin Mary (Luke 1:46–55). The fact that many of Hildegard's antiphons are long and complex has led to the suggestion that some may have been intended to frame canticles.[7]

Two types of antiphons stood on their own. Processional antiphons were, obviously, used in processions. Votive antiphons could stand alone (i.e., used for nonliturgical devotional purposes) or could be part of the liturgy; the most famous are the four Marian antiphons that came to be sung at the end of Compline on a rotating basis throughout the year. Fourteen of Hildegard's antiphons appear to fall into the category of votive antiphon; they are "much more elaborate than is customary."[8] Hildegard's antiphons are not as easy to classify as one might expect, since *differentiae*, the hallmark of a psalm antiphon, are distributed inconsistently in Dendermonde and the Riesencodex.

Although the subject matter for each of the antiphons is evident (the exception being *Karitas habundat*, an antiphon for the allegorical Charity and thus open to interpretation), the precise function of most of the antiphons (e.g., for which psalm in which Office an antiphon was intended) remains unclear. Yet a few pieces provide some guidance. Both *Et ideo puelle iste* and *O rubor sanguinis* are marked "in evangelium" in both Dendermonde and the Riesencodex, identifying them as "Gospel" antiphons. The term comes from the fact that antiphons accompanying the Benedictus and Magnificat canticles typically draw their texts from the subject of the day's Gospel. Both of Hildegard's "Gospel" antiphons deal with St. Ursula and her 11,000 Virgins, so presumably they served as the Benedictus and Magnificat antiphons for the day.

The antiphon *Studium divinitatis* provides another indication of liturgical placement. In Dendermonde it is indicated as "In matutinis laudibus"; in the Riesencodex it comes with the designation "Laudes." Each of these terms reflects medieval terminology for the Office Lauds. Further, *Studium divinitatis* is not a piece existing in isolation. It is the first of a series of eight interconnected antiphons for St. Ursula and her 11,000 Virgins, each of which has its own *differentia*. Although each antiphon is an independent musical composition—each is modally and melodically complete and can stand on its own—the eight texts are linked both syntactically and in terms of narrative.

If *Studium divinitatis* were assigned to Lauds, as the first of its five psalm antiphons, the next four in the manuscripts (*Unde quocumque venientes, De patria etiam earum, Deus enim in prima*, and *Aer enim volat*) could fill out the psalm antiphons necessary for this Office. The piece that follows these five in the manuscripts is none other than *Et ideo puelle iste*, the Gospel antiphon for St. Ursula and her 11,000 Virgins. If *Et ideo puelle iste* is in fact the Gospel antiphon for the Benedictus, it is positioned exactly where it should be, for the Lauds canticle is sung in the Office only after the five psalms and their antiphons. Interestingly, the other Gospel canticle for the feast of St. Ursula, *O rubor sanguinis*, occurs immediately before *Studium divinitatis* in the Riesencodex, suggesting that it was used as the Magnificat antiphon for First Vespers of the Ursula feast day.

The seven antiphons whose texts were first presented in *Scivias* are also noteworthy. Their appearance in the celestial concert that closes Hildegard's first theological work suggests that they, along with their corresponding responsories, are among her earlier works. As such, they are impressive achievements. Hildegard's rich poetic language (her love for superlatives evident in the opening lines of *O splendidissima gemma*, *O gloriosissimi*, and *O victoriosissimi triumphatores*) is typically supported by sweeping range (only *O splendidissima gemma* and *O pulcre facies* are less than a thirteenth in range) and not inconsequential length as well (only *O successores* and *O pulcre facies* take up fewer than eleven lines in the Riesencodex). Five of the antiphons also circulate with *differentia* (only *O gloriosissimi* and *O spectabiles viri* are missing them), with the implied repetition significantly increasing their duration.

A final antiphon to mention for its unusual qualities is the Marian votive antiphon *O tu illustrata* (see fig. 11). This work belongs to an uncommon subset of antiphons, those with verses; processional antiphons often have this feature. The work is Hildegard's only example of this kind of piece. The composition is a D-mode piece with occasional use of B-flat. It is thus striking that the work commences not on D, the same note as its final (as is most common for Hildegard's works and plainchant in general), but rather on the G above the final. It moves immediately to the A above and then reiterates that A. This opening motive is a standard Hildegard cadence (lowered seventh, final, final) no matter what mode. The motive then appears twice more in quick succession—thus, three appearances before moving to anything else. When Hildegard does break away from this, it is to go not much higher, to C, before descending to—yet again—the G–A–A motive. Only five notes in the entire first phrase ("O tu illustrata," O you, illuminated) present something other than this motive, and Hildegard has confined her range here to a mere fourth.

For the next two words, "de divina" (by divine), Hildegard provides an almost exact repeat of the first phrase, eliminating only one of the opening G–A–A motives.

This second phrase is then repeated exactly for the word "claritate" (clarity). By the end of the first six words we have thus heard the opening G–A–A ten times.

The next word, "clara" (bright), consists of yet two more G–A–A motives. Only after that does Hildegard finally send the melody somewhere else, very significantly on the phrase "virgo Maria" (Virgin Mary). That phrase itself ends with the motive C–D–D, another version of the opening gesture but now on the expected final. Hildegard has thus provided a brilliant and unique opening that insistently builds the modal tension, hammering on the fifth over and over again. Only the Virgin Mary delivers us from this constant thwarting of our melodic longing for closure. Hildegard uses rhetorical repetition in her prose writings (e.g., Letter 192, which includes "O O O," "ach ach ach" and "he he he" in close proximity) but never to the extent and power that we see at the start of *O tu illustrata*.

This bravura opening statement is only one of many melodic intricacies that inform this composition, where Hildegard's genius for melodic interconnection is on full display (two of many other examples: the key phrase "quod Eva" [because Eve] begins with the same motive as the opening; the verse commences with the motive flipped to A–A–G). Given that the entire opening would have been repeated after the verse, the performers and listeners would have experienced that delicious melodic longing yet again. This, Hildegard's longest antiphon, is truly a virtuoso effort.

Responsory

Responsories form a substantial part of Hildegard's output, making up eighteen of her seventy-seven songs. Only antiphons were more frequent in her repertoire, something true of the plainchant corpus overall. Of Hildegard's eighteen responsories, three are not given any generic designation by her scribes: *O Euchari columba* (a responsory for St. Eucharius), *O vis eternitatis* (a responsory for God), and *Rex noster* (a responsory for the Holy Innocents). All have the formal structure of responsories, however. A fourth piece, *O vos felices radices*, is designated a responsory in the Riesencodex but an antiphon in Dendermonde. It is clearly a responsory, though, as its formal structure again shows, and it is matched with the antiphon *O spectabiles viri* to form the antiphon/responsory pair for patriarchs and prophets.

Although plainchant includes numerous short responses throughout the liturgy, those that Hildegard wrote were of the type known as the "Great Responsory," or the *responsorium prolixum*. In monastic life they appeared in Matins (and sometimes Lauds and Vespers) as composed musical responses to the reading of lessons, which were themselves chanted to musically repetitive liturgical recitative. They could also function as part of processions. Usually both long and elaborate, responsories were an important site of musical creativity for Hildegard and others.

The formal elements of a typical plainchant responsory included, first, the response itself. This was followed by a verse, sung to an elaborate recitation formula, then a repeat of the response, or more often just its closing section, known as the "repetendum." This basic plan could be extended by the addition of the Lesser Doxology (usually only the first part, sung to another recitation formula) and then one more repeat of the response (again, more likely just the repetendum rather than the entire response). Not all responsories contained each of those elements, and this is true of Hildegard's creations as well.

Hildegard's responsories demonstrate considerable variety in form, range, and length; line lengths given below provide general proportions only, for scribes did not write out all of the material to be repeated but only the first word of the repetendum. The works range from the relatively short *Rex noster promptus est* for the Holy Innocents (eight lines in the Riesencodex, with a range of a tenth) to the staggering *O vos angeli* for angels, taking up nineteen lines in the Riesencodex and traversing a full two octaves and a fifth, the entire musical range known in the twelfth century. All are richly melismatic, each containing at least one phrase of twenty-five or more notes; eight works include melismas of fifty or more pitches. The limit is reached in that most extreme of works, *O vos angeli*, with one of its melismas incorporating eighty-one notes. These melismatic lengths are "exceeding by far the norms even of later medieval office repertories."[9]

Half of Hildegard's responsories use a doxology: each of the two for St. Ursula (*Favus distallans* and *Spiritui sancto honor sit*) and St. Disibod (*O felix anima* and *O viriditas digiti dei*); three of the four for Mary (*Ave Maria o auctrix*, *O clarissima mater*, and *O tu suavissima virga*), and those for God the Father (*O vis eternitatis*) and the Holy Innocents (*Rex noster promptus est*). Eight of these follow the standard medieval practice of using the first part of the doxology only: "Gloria patri et filio et spiritui sancto" (Glory be to the Father, and to the Son, and to the Holy Spirit). In one responsory, *O tu suavissima virga* (for Mary), Hildegard extends this to include "sicut erat in principio" (as it was in the beginning). In contrast to traditional chant renditions of the verse and doxology, sung to formulaic liturgical recitative, Hildegard's versions are all composed chant (as happened more often in later chant). Verse and doxology are typically related melodically and are somewhat less melismatic than the rest of the responsory.[10]

Of the nine responsories without the doxology, two have verse alone without repetenda: *O lucidissima* (for apostles) and *O nobilissima viriditas* (for virgins).

Interestingly, of the set of seven responsories whose texts appear in *Scivias* in the concert of the final vision, only one (*O tu suavissima virga*) includes a doxology, and that only in the musical sources, not *Scivias* itself.

The presence or absence of the doxology would not have been haphazard, but was rather an indication of liturgical position. Matins, the Office where Great Responsories were typically sung, was divided into a series of nocturns. According to the Benedictine Rule that governed Hildegard's community, the last responsory of each nocturn included the doxology.

Several of Hildegard's responsories appear to have served as vessels of experimentation for her. One of her two responsories for St. Disibod, *O viriditas digiti dei*, has B as its final. As noted above, B was not a pitch center recognized in the twelfth century, but Hildegard emphasizes the pitch repeatedly in the responsory by placing it at the start and finish of most phrases (her norm for modal emphasis). Perhaps this work completed an exploration of all available pitch centers for her, a project in keeping with her penchant for categorization and completeness evident in other aspects of her creativity. Other responsories exhibit her only ventures into certain modal or notational realms: *Vos flores rosarum* is her sole work based on C that uses B-natural throughout (all other C works incorporate some use of B-flat), and *O quam preciosa*, with a D center, exhibits her unique use of both B-flat and E-flat.

Two of the *Scivias* responsories (thus, earlier works) present other unusual practices for Hildegard. *O lucidissima* is a rare instance of a Hildegard composition that begins clearly in one mode but ends up just as clearly in another. It is more significant, though, for demonstrating Hildegard's most blatant use of borrowing preexistent material, in this case her own Kyrie. Various other of Hildegard's works have been identified as being influenced by other famous chants, as noted above, but in each of those instances the reminders are more subtle and rapidly fade away as her composition proceeds. With *O lucidissima*, by contrast, the borrowing cannot be missed and is, in fact, the reason that the piece commences in one modal realm but ultimately ends up in another. Quite frankly, this is not one of Hildegard's most successful works, and the overt grafting of one work onto another is an experiment she never repeated again in such an obvious manner.

Finally, the spectacular *O vos angeli* also represents something Hildegard never attempted again: an exploration of the entire written range of contemporary plainchant. One amusing note about *O vos angeli*: it is one of only two Hildegard compositions written in E that occasionally uses a B-flat. The other work? *Studium divinitatis*, her work with the narrowest range, and the only one that limits itself to the standard chant ambitus of an octave. They are a pair of extremes.

10 | Longer Genres

Alleluia

In the early medieval Mass, the alleluia was the chant immediately preceding the reading of the Gospel, though by Hildegard's time a sequence was typically inserted between the alleluia and the Gospel. A joyous chant, it was omitted during the penitential seasons of the Church year (Advent and Lent) and added to Lauds and Vespers during Easter week.[1] Structurally, the alleluia consists of an opening "alleluia" extended by a lengthy melisma, called the "jubilus," on the final syllable. This opening "alleluia" was likely sung first by a soloist and then repeated by the chorus. It was followed by a solo verse (originally a psalm verse, but other texts were eventually used as well; in any event, the text was a Proper one, changing by feast). The alleluia and jubilus were then repeated. In keeping with the joyful text, alleluias are among the most elaborate chants of the Mass, exploring wider ranges and more melismatic text setting than most other Mass chants. By the twelfth century alleluias typically exhibited many kinds of compositional planning, including the return of jubilus material at the end of the verse, beginning verse and alleluia with the same material, melodic repetition within the verse, and the use of scales and sequences. Hildegard's *Alleluia O virga mediatrix* uses some of these techniques.

The composition has the following text (the translation is literal):

Alleluia	Alleluia
O virga mediatrix	O branch, mediator,
sancta viscera tua mortem superaverunt	your holy womb overcame death
et venter tuus omnes creaturas illuminavit	and your womb illuminated all creatures
in pulchro flore	according to the beautiful flower
de suavissima integritate	arising from the most attractive purity
clausi pudoris tui orto	of your enclosed modesty.

By the twelfth century, most new alleluias were for saints or the Virgin Mary, often with "O" texts for the verses. Hildegard's verse is a Marian one, like so many of her chant texts, and could be used for any Marian Mass. Mary is the "mediary," both the medium through whom Christ was born and humanity thus saved, and the mediator who intercedes for us to her son. Christ is both her holy womb and the beautiful flower; Mary is both *virga*, branch, and *virgo*, virgin (although this latter term is not used, its implication is present, and the wordplay was common in the Middle Ages and with Hildegard), with her purity emphasized by being modified by the only superlative in the text. Hildegard uses melismas to stress alle**lu**ia, **vir**ga, media**trix**, **tu**a, **mor**tem, superave**runt**, **tu**us, illumi**na**vit, **tu**i, and **or**to, with the jubilus standing out (thirty-one notes) and the penultimate syllable even more so (forty-one notes). As we know, highlighting the next-to-last syllable through a melisma was a frequent practice of Hildegard's.

As was common in alleluias, Hildegard's opens the verse with music that is very similar to the opening "alleluia," and, as is common with her music and typical of alleluias, there are internal unifications as well—for example, "superaverunt" ends with the same music as "mediatrix"; "in pulchro" recalls "sancta viscera." These musical reminiscences reinforce the verbal cues: the mediator made it possible to overcome death; Christ is both the "holy womb" and the "beautiful flower." Chunks of repetition also appear in the final phrases: the music of "si pudoris" returns in "tui," and music from "tui or-" returns within the melisma of "orto."

This E-mode work spans an eleventh, with the lowest pitch (the D below the final) present already in the second syllable. High points are reserved for the end of the verse, cresting on the last two words, and the whole closing section of the verse, from "in pulchro flore" on, emphasizes the fifth (B) repeatedly, almost as a kind of dominant pedal, before sinking at last to the final. The work bears some resemblance to another E-mode Marian alleluia that was extremely popular at the time, the *Alleluia O Maria rubens rosa*, and Hildegard may have been influenced by that widespread work.[2]

Alleluia O virga mediatrix appears in the "long genre" section of the Riesencodex, despite its relatively short length of eight lines (the duration increased, of course, with the repetition of the initial alleluia). Many antiphons and responsories in the "short" section of the Riesencodex are considerably longer. For whatever reason, though, Hildegard's scribes copied it with the hymns and sequences.

Sequence

The other item for the Mass Proper besides the alleluia that interested Hildegard was the sequence. This was a relatively new kind of chant, first appearing in the eighth century but rapidly becoming an extremely popular venue for creativity that generated more than four thousand new melodies. Normally sung immediately before the Gospel in the Mass, sequences could also appear elsewhere in the liturgy, such as in place of the Vespers hymn. Structurally, it was most often characterized by pairs of verses (thus formally aa bb cc dd etc.); sometimes it began and/or ended with a lone verse (a bb cc . . . n). The works were substantial in length and often range as well, and text was overwhelmingly syllabic.

Beginning in the twelfth century, the texts began to be set in rhymed metric verse, generating pairs of equal duration throughout. Before that, pairs were of varying lengths: the "a" music was a different length than the "b" music, which was longer or shorter than the "c" music, and so on. This fancy new metric rhymed sequence had not yet reached the Benedictine abbeys of Rhineland Germany in Hildegard's time, though, so all of her sequences follow the older, freer pattern. Yet even if Hildegard had somehow been aware of this latest trend, it's unlikely that she would have followed it; strictly rhyming poetry was not her style.

Seven works of Hildegard's are identified as sequences in the manuscripts; various modern writers have added or subtracted to this list.[3] Of the works called sequence in Hildegard's manuscripts, one is Marian (*O virga ac diadema*) and therefore of use in any Marian Mass; one is for the Holy Spirit (*O ignis spiritus paracliti*) and hence fitting for Pentecost and possibly other occasions. The remaining five works are for specific saints and thus surely sung on their feast days, whether at Rupertsberg or elsewhere: *Columba aspexit*, for St. Maximin of Trier (January 8); *O ecclesia*, for St. Ursula (October 21); *O Euchari in leta via*, for St. Eucharius of Trier (December 8); *O ierusalem*, for St. Rupert (May 15); and *O presul vere civitatis*, for St. Disibod (July 8). Hildegard seems to have been especially fond of the very attractive *O virga ac diadema*, for the *Acta inquisitionis* reports that she would sing this while walking around the monastery, illuminated by the Holy Spirit.[4]

The sequence repertory in general favors D and G modes, but Hildegard has only one firmly in the latter (*O ierusalem*) and none in the former. Instead, she uses A (three sequences), C (two sequences), and E (one sequence). Her two sequences on C (*O presul vere civitatis* and *Columba aspexit*) sometimes use B-flats; when they do, the result is a transposed G mode. These seven works have the expanded ranges normal for her music (from a tenth to a thirteenth). More striking are their lengths. Sequences, with Hildegard's hymns, are her longest works, which is precisely what we would expect from the genre. *O ierusalem aurea civitas*, in fact, is her most expansive piece, taking up forty-two lines in the Riesencodex, and it may originally have been even longer. In one text-only manuscript it contains an entire extra strophe missing in the musical manuscripts.[5]

In terms of texting and form, Hildegard's sequences are clearly influenced by the expected norms but nonetheless retain an individuality that makes them different from sequences by others. For example, her sequences are mostly syllabic and much more so than her responsories, but they still include short melismas as well as some neumatic bits. They thus are freer in this respect than standard sequences, which are very heavily syllabic.

Hildegard shows even greater flexibility in her treatment of form. In a regular sequence, the music for a given pair of verses need only be written out once, with its two texts (one for each part of the pair) provided below the single melodic line. This would not work for any of Hildegard's sequences, for the second half of each of her pairs is always somewhat different from the first and must be written out in full. Rather than a formal structure of aa bb cc etc., then, Hildegard's forms are more properly aa' bb' cc' and so on.

For most of her sequences this inexact relationship within the couplets is not a problem; the listener (and certainly the performer) can easily hear the connections between the two sections. Three of Hildegard's sequences, though, take further liberties with our expectations. *O ignis spiritus* ends with two lone verses rather than a paired verse. *O ierusalem aurea civitas*—perhaps Hildegard's earliest effort in the genre, if it was composed in time for the Rupertsberg church consecration, as some have suggested—has two interior single verses, and its two last verses form a very lopsided pair, with the shared material tucked into the interior and end of the verses and not present at the beginnings. This sequence also begins with a triple verse rather than a paired verse. It is thus irregular in multiple respects and is, in fact, identified as a sequence only in Dendermonde, not in the Riesencodex.

The oddest of all, though, is the Ursula sequence, *O ecclesia*. Not one of its verses is clearly paired; melodic relationships, though present, are more subtle than overt, leading to many different interpretations as to the work's structure.[6] The Dendermonde manuscript and the Riesencodex even divide the text differently; in the former it is split into eleven verses, while the latter divides it into twelve. Interestingly, the Dendermonde manuscript identifies the work as a sequence, but the Riesencodex indicates only the subject matter rather than a genre. While there is a subset of the sequence known as the "aparallel sequence," such works are normally quite short, and they also date from early in the genre's history. *O ecclesia* is certainly aparallel in form, but it is neither short nor early. It is unquestionably anomalous.

Italian sequences and early sequences are typically less regular than later, northern ones, but it is unlikely that Hildegard knew Italian sequences, and completely unknown is just how many really early sequences she would have run across. What does seem clear, though, is that Hildegard's text governed her writing. Her sequence texts are filled with incredible images (e.g., the goat walks with the elephant in *Columba aspexit*), with components appearing in multiple works (e.g., jewels, the dawn, the smoke of incense). Hildegard makes no attempt to fit her Latin into the straitjacket that a strict sequence form would require. In fact, in all of her many pairs, only one presents exactly the same number of syllables in each half: the final pair in *O presul vere civitatis*. Every other pair is uneven in length, meaning that her texts preclude formal regularity. Thus, her poetic style prevents her acquiescence to strict generic norms.

Yet it is precisely this lack of precision that makes her sequences so fascinating to hear and to perform. With the exceptions noted above, they are comprised of musically unified pairs whose variations keep us constantly engaged. Just as irregularities in the texture of a fabric provide changes of light and hold our interest, so, too, do Hildegard's constant minor changes of pitch, direction, and duration keep us on our toes aurally. The delicious variety of each half of a pair—the constantly shifting, subtle inflections—make these pieces some of Hildegard's most compelling.

Hildegard uses varied repetition to create cohesion over a large span. In *Columba aspexit*, for example, the formal structure is aa' bb' cc' dd' e. The a/a' and c/c' sections each begin with the same melodic turn (C–D–C) while the b/b' and d/d' sections share their own melodic incipit (C–E–F–G). In contrast, the "e" verse commences with an upward leap of a fifth, immediately signaling that this section is something different (the conclusion, as it turns out).

Range is another device that Hildegard employs to provide direction. The magnificent *O presul vere civitatis* provides a powerful example here (see fig. 10, beginning with the top staff). The work is on C, extending in an expansive range from the E below middle C to an octave above middle C—thus almost two full octaves. The composition begins on middle C and at first hovers there or below, but slowly rises to reach ever higher pitches. With the exception of brief forays to high C in the third pair of verses, however, the work does not extend above G in the first four pairs. Then we get the fifth and penultimate pair of verses, where we have the following text:

[In alto stas	You [Disibod] stand on high
non erubescens] [ante Deum vivum]	not blushing before the living God
[et protegis viridi rore]	and you protect with refreshing dew
[laudantes deum ista voce]	those praising God with this voice:
[O dulcis vita	"O sweet life
et o beata] [perseverantia	and o blessed perseverance
que in] hoc beato Disibodo	in this blessed Disibod
gloriosum lumen [semper edificasti	you built a glorious light forever
in celesti Ierusalem]	in celestial Jerusalem."

Here Hildegard begins an inexorable drive to the work's climax. Over and over she repeats a variant of the same phrase, beginning on middle C, leaping up to F, rising to B (and once high C), and then descending to circle around a pause on G. Brackets in the Latin text above show where these slightly varied but closely unified phrases occur: six times before "hoc beato Disibodo." This ceaseless repetition powerfully builds the tension, with its rise and then fall to G, heard (even then, not just now) as an incomplete resting place, not the expected final. Suddenly at the end of the sixth phrase, "perseverantia que in" (blessed perseverance indeed!) we know that something different is about to happen, for on the final word, "in," Hildegard breaks with her previous pattern. Instead of moving from F to G—the closing move for the previous five phrases—she goes instead from F down to D, a note conspicuously absent from this pair of verses. This is a favorite Hildegard trick—to avoid the use of one pitch for an extended period and then to introduce it as an aural shock heralding some kind of structural change.

The introduction of D prepares us for the climactic phrase "hoc beato Disibodo gloriosum lumen" (this blessed Disibod a glorious light). Rising by step now rather than leap, the melody climbs up from F to high C, cresting exactly as the word "Disibodo" begins and then descending sequentially C–B–A–G, B–A–G–F, coming to rest on G again. The verse ends with one more appearance of the repeated phrase, and Hildegard then closes the sequence with a greatly subdued final pair consistently pitched in a lower range.

Hildegard may have had mixed feelings about her former monastery, but its patron saint inspired a very fine work. And it is perhaps telling that the musical climax of the composition comes not just on the word "Disibod" but also in the verse that gives the words of those under his protection: surely these are the monks of Disibodenberg invoked here. We can see this sequence, then, as a musical gift and possibly even a gesture of forgiveness to those on whom Hildegard once depended.

Hymn

Hildegard wrote four pieces that her scribes identified as hymns. These could have been used in the Divine Office (every service included a hymn) or in processions. Like her sequences, two belong to Mary and the Holy Spirit (*Ave generosa* and *O ignee spiritus*, respectively). The other two are for saints: Ursula again (*Cum vox sanguinis*) and St. Matthias (*Mathias sanctus*).

The normal medieval hymn was strophic with a metrical text, frequently of four predominantly syllabic lines of equal length. The final strophe usually paraphrased the Lesser Doxology and typically ended with an "amen." Processional hymns often had a refrain. Many hymns were through-composed, with the highest pitch reached in the third line. Early hymns were often in a narrow, modally ambiguous range; later ones expanded the range and were clearer tonally. In the overall hymn repertory, some melodies are used for many texts, and some texts generated many melodies.

Hildegard's hymns (all identified as such in all sources) match these standards only approximately. While each text is divided into multiple sections, indicated by rubrication in the manuscripts, these are strophes in name only. As with her sequences, all the music for all text is written out, since the exact repetition we would expect with a true strophic composition is missing. Each work contains strophes/sections of wildly different lengths, and metric regularity is completely absent. Given that such regularity is anathema to Hildegard, it's no surprise that her hymns are the most distant of her works in terms of generic expectations.

Also like the sequences, the works are long, ranging from seven sections (*Ave generosa*, taking up nineteen lines in the Riesencodex) to thirteen sections

(*O ignee spiritus*, thirty-one lines in the Riesencodex and the longest of all Hildegard's works save for the sequence *O ierusalem*). The ranges are expansive, too (eleventh, twelfth, thirteenth, fourteenth). Further, they share a predilection for syllabic text-setting, even if they sometimes include short melismas as well. Thus, even if (like the sequences) they are not as syllabic as one would expect for the genre, they are still more syllabic than Hildegard's other genres and thus akin to normal hymns in that respect.

The works contain numerous examples of small-scale motivic unification. *O ignee spiritus* is reminiscent of *Columba aspexit* in opening all but one of its sections with one of two possible motives. *Ave generosa* opens all sections but one with the same rising fifth; most of the strophes in *Cum vox sanguinis* begin the same way. Other unifying motives appear internally in these three works. *Mathias sanctus*, though, stands in dramatic contrast here, for it represents a kind of generic hybrid. Its formal structure is readily diagrammed as aa' bb' cc' dd' e—in other words, that of a sequence, even though it is labeled a hymn in the Riesencodex, its only source. Sequences, though, were not normally sung during Lent, and the feast day for St. Matthias is February 24, which frequently falls during Lent. And *Mathias sanctus* concludes like the other works called hymns. While none of Hildegard's hymns paraphrases the doxology in its closing section, each begins that section with a "Nunc" phrase, three of them remarkably alike: "Nunc omnis ecclesia in gaudio rutilet" (now let the whole church blush in gladness) in *Ave generosa*; "Nunc ergo gaudeat omnis ecclesia" (now therefore let the whole church rejoice) in *Mathias sanctus*; "Nunc gaudeant omnes celi" (now let all the heavens rejoice) in *Cum vox sanguinis*; "Nunc dignare nos omnes" (now deign [to gather] us all) in *O ignee spiritus*). "Nunc" is a favorite word of Hildegard's, but the similarity of these closing phrases is striking and surely intentional. Further, each hymn ends with the "amen" expected for the genre (a pleasing melismatic contrast to the preceding material), a conclusion not found in Hildegard's other compositions. Thus, while Hildegard's hymns provide a very inexact match with contemporary works of that name, they display a type of logic suggesting that Hildegard had her own fairly definite ideas of what she wanted for a piece bearing that name.

In the case of *Mathias sanctus*, then, Hildegard appears to have written a multipurpose work. Minus its "amen," which is musically independent, it looks like Hildegard's other sequences and could have functioned as such in the years when St. Matthias's feast day fell outside of Lent. With the "amen," *Mathias sanctus* would take its place as a hymn when, as was frequently the case, February 24 arrived during Lent.

Symphonia

Despite not being a liturgical genre, the term "symphonia" is used by Hildegard's scribes to identify two of her compositions. *O dulcissime amator* and *O pater omnium* are signaled respectively in the manuscripts as "Symphonia virginum" (symphony of virgins, in both manuscripts) and "Symphonia viduarum" (symphony of widows; the piece appears in both collections but received its title only in the Dendermonde copy). In the Middle Ages the word "symphonia" had several related meanings, including consonance, concord, harmony, and agreement of sounds, and could be used to designate polyphony. The term was also used to indicate several musical instruments, especially those that could play more than one note simultaneously—most frequently the hurdy-gurdy (an instrument thought by some to be of monastic origin and used to learn plainchant). Hildegard herself displayed the word most obviously in the phrase "Symphonia armonie celestium revelationum," commonly assumed to be her name for her collected songs, but the term also appears in various places throughout her writings and in her chant texts as well (e.g., in *Ave generosa*, where the church is to "in symphonia sonet," resound in harmony). In one instance she turns it into a verb: "in te symphonizat spiritus sanctus" (in you the Holy Spirit "symphonizes," makes harmony) in her sequence *O ierusalem*. Hildegard evidently uses it in her many citations to refer not to any instrument but rather to the sense of concord or harmonious sound.

The two constituencies named in these symphoniae are the same two who made up Hildegard's community: virgins and widows—the celibate. Virgins are the obvious members of any monastic community, but widows (and widowers) could also take religious vows. Indeed, successive crusades throughout the Middle Ages generated a plethora of widows, some of whom retreated to monasteries (the First Crusade began in 1095; the Second in 1144). In Hildegard's eyes, though, virgins outranked widows, and her two symphoniae are different in numerous ways.

The lengthy text of *O dulcissime amator*, the "symphony of virgins," draws on the standard medieval imagery of Christ as bridegroom, with its overtones of the Song of Songs: "O sweetest lover" (O dulcissime amator), "bridegroom and comforter" (sponsum et consolatorem), "we are married to you" (copulate sumus tibi), "we embrace you" (amplectimur te), "sweetest bridegroom" (dulcissime sponse). *O pater omnium* uses a shorter text that speaks directly to the status of widows: "we relinquished a fertile lover in marriage" (reliquimus . . . fertilem amatorem coniunctionis), "we are married to you in a different way" (in altera vice copulate sumus tibi). The longer text of *O dulcissime amator* generates a significantly longer setting than that of *O pater omnium*—twenty-three versus fifteen lines in the Riesencodex—thus providing a greater emphasis on virginity.

The two works are linked via a common final, E, Hildegard's favorite, but position themselves differently around that final, with *O pater omnium* lying slightly lower in the range than *O dulcissime amator*. In fact, *O pater omnium* reaches the very lowest note available in medieval notation of the twelfth century, the low G more than an octave below middle C. As noted previously, fixed pitch did not exist during the Middle Ages, and singers (whether male or female) would simply have sung a piece of chant wherever it lay comfortably in their voices. Nonetheless, use of the lowest notated pitch generates an interesting symbolism for widows, whose sexual experience tied them more closely to the physical world than ethereal virgins; they were simply more earthbound. On another symbolic note, widowhood represents an older stage of life than virginity, and the mature voice typically deepens.

In addition to lying lower and being shorter overall than *O dulcissime amator*, *O pater omnium* is in other ways more sober than the "symphony of virgins." Its text setting is frequently syllabic, with few melismas (only five overall) and those rather limited in scope (the longest, only eight notes, is on the "vir" of "virga," branch). *O dulcissime amator*, in contrast, sports thirteen melismas, the longest of which (on "deliciarum," delights) runs on for sixteen pitches. *O pater omnium* has numerous repeated notes and a recitative-like quality, almost sounding as if it were derived from a psalm tone. Simply put, it would be easier to sing than *O dulcissime amator*, which is more freewheeling in its melodic lines. That Hildegard would provide the simpler work for widows to sing is actually quite practical. Joining Hildegard's community only after married life, widows would not have had years of singing plainchant in the daily Offices for hours at a time. They would instead be new to the performance of chant in general, and Hildegard's ofttimes challenging music in particular. Hildegard thus took their lesser musical experience into account when writing the widows' symphony.

Unassigned

The song *O viridissima virga* appears only in the Riesencodex, where it lacks a generic assignment. This work, a poetic paean to the Virgin Mary, traverses the limited range of a tenth and is a rare G-mode composition. It has been suggested as a sequence for various reasons.[7] At seventeen manuscript staves it appears in the "long" section of the Riesencodex, where it is preceded by the Marian sequence

O virga ac diadema and followed by the Marian hymn *Ave generosa*. Rubrication in the manuscript divides the work into eight sections. These eight do not fall into the melodic pairs expected of sequences (though that was the case with certain sequences as well), and several of *O viridissima virga*'s sections share at least similar opening motives: verses 1, 2, and 6; 3 and 8; and 4 and 7. As with a sequence, the text is heavily syllabic, with melismas restricted to the significant words "balsami" (balsam), "plena" (full), and "altissimo" (highest), this last the closing word of the composition. Yet Hildegard already had a sequence for the Virgin Mary, one that was apparently a personal favorite, and in none of her longer genres does she duplicate recipients. It is likely, then, that the lack of generic designation was intentional.

––––––––

The function of Hildegard's songs as components, for the most part, of her monastic liturgy was complemented by other functions that the songs (and *Ordo virtutum*) served as well. They are yet one more expression of her theological interpretations, and as such they serve as tools for the enlightenment and inspiration of her own nuns, but also of anyone who would encounter the songs. Certainly that would include the monks of Villers and Disibodenberg, probably those of the various Trier monasteries whose patron saints Hildegard celebrated, and ultimately anyone who consulted the Riesencodex, its copies, or any manuscript that contained the text of a song, such as the manuscripts for *Scivias*. Finally, again and again, the songs serve as vehicles of praise for God the Father, Son, and Holy Spirit; for the Virgin Mary; for martyrs and apostles and confessors and innocents and saints; and for all those whom she celebrates in her words and music. Even had it lacked a fixed function in the Church year, Hildegard's music was a cry of joy with her boundless love for the Church in all its glory and all its components. No matter what our individual religious beliefs are, it remains a cry of joy for us today as well.

LIST OF WORKS

Musical Works

DRAMA

Ordo virtutum (The Play of the Virtues)

SYMPHONIA ARMONIE CELESTIUM REVELATIONUM (SYMPHONY OF THE HARMONY OF THE CELESTIAL REVELATIONS)

Final	B♭[1]	Title (genre and subject)
E		Aer enim volat (antiphon for St. Ursula and the 11,000 Virgins)
E		Alleluia O virga mediatrix (alleluia for Mary)
A	♭	Ave generosa (hymn for Mary)
C	♭	Ave Maria o auctrix (responsory for Mary)
C	♭	Columba aspexit (sequence for St. Maximinus)
E		Cum erubuerint infelices (antiphon for Mary)
E		Cum processit factura (antiphon for Mary)
A	♭	Cum vox sanguinis (hymn for St. Ursula and the 11,000 Virgins)
D	♭	De patria etiam earum (antiphon for St. Ursula and the 11,000 Virgins)
E		Deus enim in prima muliere (antiphon for St. Ursula and the 11,000 Virgins)
E		Deus enim rorem (antiphon for St. Ursula and the 11,000 Virgins)
A	♭	Et ideo puelle iste (antiphon "in evangelium" for St. Ursula and the 11,000 Virgins)
A	♭	Favus distallans (responsory for the 11,000 Virgins)
C	♭	Hodie aperuit nobis (antiphon for Mary)
D	♭	Karitas habundat (antiphon for Caritas)
F	♭	Kyrie eleyson (Kyrie)
E		Laus trinitati (antiphon for the Trinity)
C	♭	Mathias sanctus (hymn/[sequence][2] for St. Matthias)
C	♭	Nunc gaudeant materna viscera ([antiphon] for the dedication of a church)

126

A		O beata infantia (antiphon for St. Disibod)
D	♭	O beatissime Ruperte (antiphon for St. Rupert)
A	♭	O Bonifaci ([antiphon] for St. Boniface)
G	♭	O chohors milicie floris (antiphon for apostles)
A	♭	O choruscans lux stellarum ([antiphon] for the dedication of a church)
C	♭	O clarissima mater (responsory for Mary)
D³	♭	O cruor sanguinis (antiphon for Christ; incomplete)
E		O dulcis electe (responsory for St. John the Evangelist)
E⁴		O dulcissime amator (symphonia of virgins)
A	♭	O ecclesia (sequence for the 11,000 Virgins)
E		O eterne deus (antiphon for God the Father)
E		O Euchari columba ([responsory] for St. Eucharius)
E		O Euchari in leta via (sequence for St. Eucharius)
E		O felix anima (responsory for St. Disibod)
E		O felix apparicio (antiphon for St. Rupert)
D	♭	O frondens virga (antiphon for Mary)
E		O gloriosissimi lux vivens angeli (antiphon for angels)
G		O ierusalem aurea civitas (sequence for St. Rupert)
D	♭	O ignee spiritus (hymn for the Holy Spirit)
A	♭	O ignis spiritus paracliti (sequence for the Holy Spirit)
G	♭	O lucidissima apostolorum turba (responsory for apostles)
A	♭	O magne pater (antiphon for God the Father)
E		O mirum admirandum (antiphon for St. Disibod)
C	♭	O nobilissima viriditas (responsory for virgins)
E		O orzchis ecclesia ([antiphon] for the dedication of a church)
D		O pastor animarum (antiphon for God the Father)
E		O pater omnium (symphonia of widows)
C	♭	O presul vere civitatis (sequence for St. Disibod)
E		O pulcre facies (antiphon for virgins)
E		O quam magnum miraculum (antiphon for Mary)
C	♭	O quam mirabilis (antiphon for God the Father)
D	♭/♭⁵	O quam preciosa (responsory for Mary)
D	♭	O rubor sanguinis (antiphon "in evangelium" for the 11,000 Virgins)
E		O spectabiles viri ([antiphon] for patriarchs and prophets)
E		O speculum columbe (antiphon for St. John the Evangelist)
E		O splendidissima gemma (antiphon for Mary)
D	♭	O successores (antiphon for confessors)
D	♭	O tu illustrata (antiphon with verse for Mary)
A	♭	O tu suavissima virga (responsory for Mary)
E		O victoriosissimi triumphatores (antiphon for martyrs)
A	♭	O virga ac diadema (sequence for Mary)
E		O virgo ecclesia ([antiphon] for the dedication of a Church)
G		O viridissima virga (song for Mary)
B		O viriditas digiti dei (responsory for St. Disibod)
E		O virtus sapientie (antiphon for Wisdom/the Trinity)

E		O vis eternitatis ([responsory] for God the Father and Son)
E	♭	O vos angeli (responsory for angels)
E		O vos felices radices (responsory for patriarchs and prophets)
C	♭	O vos imitatores (responsory for confessors)
E		Quia ergo femina (antiphon for Mary)
E		Quia felix puericia (antiphon for St. Rupert)
E		Rex noster promptus est ([responsory] for the Holy Innocents)
D		Sed diabolus (antiphon for St. Ursula and the 11,000 Virgins)
A	♭	Spiritui sancto honor sit (responsory for the 11,000 Virgins)
A	♭	Spiritus sanctus vivificans vita (antiphon for the Holy Spirit)
E	♭	Studium divinitatis ([antiphon] "in matutinis laudibus" [Dendermonde]/ "Laudes" [Riesencodex] for St. Ursula and the 11,000 Virgins)
D/A?[6]	♭	Unde quocumque venientes (antiphon for St. Ursula and the 11,000 Virgins)
C		Vos flores rosarum (responsory for martyrs)

LOST COMPOSITIONS?

O factura dei (for humanity)
O fili dilectissime (for Christ by Mary)
O magna res (for Mary)
O verbum patris (for God the Father)

Prose Works

THE THEOLOGICAL TRILOGY

Scivias (Know the Ways)
Liber vite meritorum (The Book of Life's Merits)
Liber divinorum operum/De operacione dei (The Book of Divine Works/On the Workings of God)

HAGIOGRAPHY

Vita Sancti Ruperti, Confessoris (Life of St. Rupert, Confessor)
Vita Sancti Disibodi, Episcopi (Life of St. Disibod, Bishop)

OTHER THEOLOGICAL WORKS

De regula Sancti Benedicti (On the Benedictine Rule)
Explanatio symboli Sancti Athanasii (Explanation of the Athanasian Creed)
Expositiones evangeliorum (Homilies on the Gospels)
Solutiones triginta octo quaestionum (Answers to Thirty-Eight Questions)

SCIENTIFIC WORKS

Physica/Liber simplicis medicinae (The Book of Simple Medicine)
Cause et cure/Liber compositae medicinae (Causes and Cures/The Book of Compound Medicine)

OTHER WORKS

Correspondence
Lingua ignota (Unknown Language)
Litterae ignotae (Unknown Letters)

NOTES

Chapter 1. Before Rupertsberg

1. Rare exceptions exist; poet-composer Guillaume de Machaut comes to mind.

2. In citing Hildegard's texts throughout this book I have followed the standard (but not universal) practice of spelling the *e caudata* (e with right-facing hook below) as "e" rather than "ae."

3. All references to Hildegard's vita are taken from the translation in Anna Silvas, *Jutta and Hildegard: The Biographical Sources*, Medieval Women: Texts and Contexts 1 (Turnhout, Belgium: Brepols, 1998), 135–210.

4. Ibid., 209.

5. Ibid., 158.

6. Recounted at the beginning of *Scivias*, discussed below.

7. Silvas, *Jutta and Hildegard*, 267.

8. For example, see Hildegard's statement in Letter 31r about the "True Light" (Holy Spirit) in *The Letters of Hildegard of Bingen*, 3 vols., trans. Joseph L. Baird and Radd K. Ehrman (New York: Oxford University Press, 1994–2004), 1: 95.

9. Silvas, *Jutta and Hildegard*, 103.

10. Ibid., 19.

11. *Letters of Hildegard*, 1:155.

12. Silvas, *Jutta and Hildegard*, 69 and 214.

13. Ibid., 108.

14. Ibid., 106.

15. Ibid., 108.

16. Ibid., 71.

17. Ibid.

18. Ibid., 73.

19. Ibid., 109.

20. Ibid., 109–110.

21. Ibid., 24.

22. Ibid., 71.

23. Ibid., 160.

24. Ibid., 139.

25. Ibid., 139.

26. Ibid., 79.

27. Ibid., 80.

28. Ibid., 81.

29. Ibid., 83.

30. Hildegard of Bingen, *Scivias*, trans. Mother Columba Hart and Jane Bishop, intro. Barbara J. Newman, preface Caroline Walker Bynum (New York: Paulist Press, 1990), 59.

31. Ibid.

32. Ibid.

33. Ibid., 59–61.

34. Letters refer to the numbering used in *The Letters of Hildegard*. The dating here is from John Van Engen, "Letters and the Public *Persona* of Hildegard," in *Hildegard von Bingen in ihrem historischen Umfeld: Internationaler wissenschaftlicher Kongreß zum 900jährigen Jubiläum, 13.–19. September 1998, Bingen am Rhein*, ed. Alfred Haverkamp (Mainz: Verlag Philipp von Zabern, 2000), 381.

35. Barbara Newman, "Hildegard and Her Hagiographers: The Remaking of Female Sainthood," in *Gendered Voices: Medieval Saints and Their Interpreters*, ed. Catherine M. Mooney (Philadelphia: University of Pennsylvania Press, 1999), 22.

36. See Van Engen, "Letters and the Public *Persona*," 379–92.

37. Silvas, *Jutta and Hildegard*, 37–39.

38. Beverly Mayne Kienzle, *Hildegard and Her Gospel Homilies: Speaking New Mysteries*, Medieval Women: Texts and Contexts 12 (Turnhout, Belgium: Brepols, 2009), 37.

39. Silvas, *Jutta and Hildegard*, 144.

40. Ibid., 101.

41. Constant J. Mews, "Hildegard and the Schools," in *Hildegard of Bingen: The Context of Her Thought and Art*, ed. Charles Burnett and Peter Dronke (London: Warburg Institute, 1998), 94.

Chapter 2. A New Life

1. Hildegard of Bingen, *The Letters of Hildegard of Bingen*, 3 vols., trans. Joseph L. Baird and Radd K. Ehrman (New York: Oxford University Press, 1994–2004), Letter 234; see also Letters 198 and 249.

2. Anna Silvas, *Jutta and Hildegard: The Biographical Sources*. Medieval Women: Texts and Contexts 1 (Turnhout, Belgium: Brepols, 1998), 106.

3. Ibid., 160.

4. Ibid., 164.

5. The date is often given erroneously as 1152.

6. Madeline Caviness, "Artist: To See, Hear, and Know All at Once," in *Voice of the Living Light: Hildegard of Bingen and Her World*, ed. Barbara Newman (Berkeley: University of California Press, 1998), 120.

7. See Barbara Newman, *Sister of Wisdom: St. Hildegard's Theology of the Feminine*, 2nd ed. (Berkeley: University of California Press, 1997).

8. On these works and the church dedication, see Honey Meconi, "Hildegard's *Lingua ignota* and Music," in *Musik des Mittelalters und der Renaissance: Festschrift Klaus-Jürgen*

Sachs zum 80. Geburtstag, ed. Rainer Kleinertz, Christoph Flamm, and Wolf Frobenius, Veröffentlichungen des Staatlichen Instituts für Musikforschung 18, Studien zur Geschichte der Musiktheorie 8 (Hildesheim, Germany: Georg Olms Verlag, 2010), 59–79.

9. See Meconi, "Hildegard's *Lingua ignota*."

10. Translation by Honey Meconi.

11. See Meconi, "Hildegard's *Lingua ignota*," 67.

12. Newman, *Sister of Wisdom*, 237.

13. The most recent discussion of the precedence of the musical version is in Margot E. Fassler, "Allegorical Architecture in *Scivias*: Hildegard's Setting for the *Ordo Virtutum*," *Journal of the American Musicological Society* 67 (2014): 317–78.

14. Marianne Richert Pfau and Stefan J. Morent, *Hildegard von Bingen: Der Klang des Himmels*, Europäische Komponistinnen 1 (Cologne: Böhlau Verlag, 2005), 227–52.

15. The importance of Humility for Hildegard is likely derived from both the Rule of Benedict and the writings of Bernard of Clairvaux; see Gunilla Iversen, "*Ego Humilitatis, regina Virtutum*: Poetic Language and Literary Structure in Hildegard of Bingen's Vision of the Virtues," in *The Ordo Virtutum of Hildegard of Bingen: Critical Studies*, ed. Audrey Ekdahl Davidson, Early Drama, Art, and Music Monograph Series 18 (Kalamazoo, MI: Medieval Institute Publications, 1992), 79–110.

16. See Peter Dronke, ed., *Nine Medieval Latin Plays*, Cambridge Medieval Latin Plays 1 (Cambridge, UK: Cambridge University Press, 1994), 152–55.

17. Hildegard of Bingen, *Scivias*, trans. Mother Columba Hart and Jane Bishop, intro. Barbara J. Newman, preface Caroline Walker Bynum (New York: Paulist Press, 1990), 415.

18. Constant J. Mews, "Hildegard, the Speculum Virginum and Religious Reform in the Twelfth Century," in *Hildegard von Bingen in ihrem historischen Umfeld: Internationaler wissenschaftlicher Kongreß zum 900jährigen Jubiläum, 13.–19. September 1998, Bingen am Rhein*, ed. Alfred Haverkamp (Mainz, Germany: Verlag Philipp von Zabern, 2000), 266.

19. Robert Potter, "The *Ordo Virtutum*: Ancestor of the English Moralities?" in Davidson, *Ordo Virtutum of Hildegard of Bingen*, 31–41.

20. Bruce W. Hozeski, "The Parallel Patterns in Hrotsvitha of Gandersheim, a Tenth Century German Playwright, and in Hildegard of Bingen, a Twelfth Century German Playwright," *Annuale Mediaevale* 16 (1977): 42–53.

21. Peter Dronke, *Poetic Individuality in the Middle Ages: New Departures in Poetry, 1000–1150*, 2nd ed. (Oxford: Oxford University Press, 1986), xxxvii–xxxix.

22. Bruce W. Hozeski, "Parallel Patterns in Prudentius's *Psychomachia* and Hildegard of Bingen's *Ordo Virtutum*," *14th Century English Mystics Newsletter* 8 (1982): 8–20.

23. Ulrike Wiethaus, "Cathar Influences in Hildegard of Bingen's Play 'Ordo Virtutum,'" *American Benedictine Review* 38 (1987): 192–203.

24. Julia Bolton Holloway, "The Monastic Context of Hildegard's *Ordo Virtutum*," in Davidson, *Ordo Virtutum of Hildegard of Bingen*, 63–77.

25. Pamela Sheingorn, "The Virtues of Hildegard's *Ordo Virtutum*, or, It *Was* a Woman's World," in Davidson, *Ordo Virtutum of Hildegard of Bingen*, 43–62.

26. Potter, "*Ordo Virtutum*," 36.

27. Roswitha Dabke, "The Hidden Scheme of the Virtues in Hildegard of Bingen's *Ordo Virtutum*," *Parergon* 23 (2006): 11–46.

28. Margot Fassler, "Music for the Love Feast: Hildegard of Bingen and the Song of Songs," in *Resonant Witness: Conversations between Music and Theology*, ed. Jeremy S. Begbie and Steven R. Guthrie (Grand Rapids, MI: William B. Eerdmans, 2011), 355–81. See also Fassler's interpretation in Fassler, "Allegorical Architecture in *Scivias*."

29. Tova Leigh-Choate, William T. Flynn, and Margot E. Fassler, "Hearing the Heavenly Symphony: An Overview of Hildegard's Musical Oeuvre with Case Studies," in *A Companion to Hildegard of Bingen*, ed. Beverly Mayne Kienzle, Debra L. Stoudt, and George Ferzoco, Brill's Companions to the Christian Tradition 45 (Leiden: Brill, 2014), at 174.

30. Pfau and Morent, *Hildegard von Bingen*, 224–26.

Chapter 3. New Challenges

1. Anna Silvas, *Jutta and Hildegard: The Biographical Sources*, Medieval Women: Texts and Contexts 1 (Turnhout, Belgium: Brepols, 1998), 112.

2. The reference is to Jesus's cry on the cross, "My God, my God, why hast thou forsaken me?" appearing in both Matthew 27:46 and Mark 15:34.

3. *The Letters of Hildegard of Bingen*, 3 vols., trans. Joseph L. Baird and Radd K. Ehrman (New York: Oxford University Press, 1994–2004), 1:50.

4. Julia Bolton Holloway, "The Monastic Context of Hildegard's *Ordo Virtutum*," in *The Ordo Virtutum of Hildegard of Bingen: Critical Studies*, ed. Audrey Ekdahl Davidson, Early Drama, Art, and Music Monograph Series 18 (Kalamazoo, MI: Medieval Institute Publications, 1992), 70–72; Robert Potter, "The *Ordo Virtutum*: Ancestor of the English Moralities?" in Davidson, *Ordo Virtutum of Hildegard of Bingen*, 37.

5. Gunilla Iversen, "Réalizer une vision: La dernière vision de *Scivias* et le drame *Ordo Virtutum* de Hildegarde de Bingen," *Revue de musicologie* 86 (2000): 37–63.

6. Susan Schibanoff, "Hildegard of Bingen and Richardis of Stade: The Discourse of Desire," in *Same Sex Love and Desire among Women in the Middle Ages*, ed. Francesca Canadé Sautman and Pamela Sheingorn (New York: Palgrave, 2001), 49–83.

7. Constant J. Mews, "Hildegard and the Schools," in *Hildegard of Bingen: The Context of Her Thought and Art*, ed. Charles Burnett and Peter Dronke (London: Warburg Institute, 1998), 96–97.

8. Silvas, *Jutta and Hildegard*, 131.

9. Mews, "Hildegard and the Schools," 94–96.

10. *Letters of Hildegard of Bingen*, 1:127.

11. Madeline H. Caviness, "Hildegard as Designer of the Illustrations to Her Works," in Burnett and Dronke, *Hildegard of Bingen: The Context of Her Thought and Art*, 38–40.

12. Hildegard of Bingen, *Scivias*, trans. Mother Columba Hart and Jane Bishop, intro. Barbara J. Newman, preface Caroline Walker Bynum (New York: Paulist Press, 1990), 201.

13. Hans-Jürgen Kotzur, ed., *Hildegard von Bingen 1098–1179* (Mainz, Germany: Verlag Philipp von Zabern, 1998), 104–107.

14. Barbara Newman, "Hildegard and Her Hagiographers: The Remaking of Female Sainthood," in *Gendered Voices: Medieval Saints and Their Interpreters*, ed. Catherine M. Mooney (Philadelphia: University of Pennsylvania Press, 1999), 201.

15. Silvas, *Jutta and Hildegard*, 27.

16. Tova Leigh-Choate, William T. Flynn, and Margot E. Fassler, "Hearing the Heavenly Symphony: An Overview of Hildegard's Musical Oeuvre with Case Studies," in *A Companion to Hildegard of Bingen*, ed. Beverly Mayne Kienzle, Debra L. Stoudt, and George Ferzoco, Brill's Companions to the Christian Tradition 45 (Leiden: Brill, 2014), 175.

17. Saint Hildegard of Bingen, *Symphonia: A Critical Edition of the Symphonia armonie celestium revelationum [Symphony of the Harmony of Celestial Revelations]*, 2nd ed., introduction, translations, and commentary by Barbara Newman (Ithaca, NY: Cornell University Press, 1998), 310.

18. *Letters of Hildegard of Bingen*, 1:162–63.

19. Ibid., 2:171, in Letter 195r.

20. Lieven Van Acker, "Der Briefwechsel der heiligen Hildegard von Bingen: Vorbemerkungen zu einer kritischen Edition," *Revue bénédictine* 98 (1988): 162–63.

21. Silvas, *Jutta and Hildegard*, 245.

Chapter 4. New Creations

1. Hildegard of Bingen, *Scivias*, trans. Mother Columba Hart and Jane Bishop, intro. Barbara J. Newman, preface Caroline Walker Bynum (New York: Paulist Press, 1990), 67. Some writers attribute Hildegard's visions to migraines. If so, they were surely the most inspirational migraines in human history.

2. Madeline H. Caviness, *Art in the Medieval West and Its Audience* (Aldershot: Ashgate, 2001), xvii–xxi.

3. See Madeline H. Caviness, "Hildegard as Designer of the Illustrations to Her Works," in *Hildegard of Bingen: The Context of Her Thought and Art*, ed. Charles Burnett and Peter Dronke (London: Warburg Institute, 1998).

4. Margot Fassler, "Hildegard's Cosmos and Its Music: Making a Digital Model for the Modern Planetarium," AMS President's Endowed Plenary Lecture, Annual Meeting of the American Musicological Society, Milwaukee, November 6, 2014.

5. Michael Embach, "Hildegard of Bingen (1098–1179): A History of Reception," in *A Companion to Hildegard of Bingen*, ed. Beverly Mayne Kienzle, Debra L. Stoudt, and George Ferzoco, Brill's Companions to the Christian Tradition 45 (Leiden: Brill, 2014), 274.

6. Hildegard, *Scivias*, trans. Hart and Bishop, 525.

7. Ibid., 526.

8. Ibid., 528.

9. Ibid., 528–29.

10. Ibid., 532–34.

11. John Van Engen, "Letters and the Public *Persona* of Hildegard," in *Hildegard von Bingen in ihrem historischen Umfeld: Internationaler wissenschaftlicher Kongreß zum 900jährigen Jubiläum, 13.–19. September 1998, Bingen am Rhein*, ed. Alfred Haverkamp (Mainz, Germany: Verlag Philipp von Zabern, 2000), 376.

12. See the discussion in Honey Meconi, "Hildegard's *Lingua ignota* and Music," in *Musik des Mittelalters und der Renaissance: Festschrift Klaus-Jürgen Sachs zum 80. Geburtstag*, ed. Rainer Kleinertz, Christoph Flamm, and Wolf Frobenius, Veröffentlichungen des Staatlichen Instituts für Musikforschung 18, Studien zur Geschichte der Musiktheorie 8 (Hildesheim, Germany: Georg Olms Verlag, 2010), 60.

13. Florence Eliza Glaze, "Medical Writer: 'Behold the Human Creature,'" in *Voice of the Living Light: Hildegard of Bingen and Her World*, ed. Barbara Newman (Berkeley: University of California Press, 1998), 145.

14. *Hildegard von Bingen's Physica: The Complete English Translation of Her Classic Work on Health and Healing*, trans. Priscilla Throop (Rochester, VT: Healing Arts Press, 1998), 225.

15. Constant J. Mews, "Hildegard and the Schools," in Burnett and Dronke, *Hildegard of Bingen*, 99.

16. Hildegard of Bingen, *Holistic Healing*, trans. Patrick Madigan, ed. Mary Palmquist and John Kulas (Collegeville, MN: Liturgical Press, 1994), 210.

17. Ibid., 9.

18. Ibid., 80.

19. Unless these instructions were intended to counter "amenorrhea brought on by malnutrition," as suggested by Sabina Flanagan, *Hildegard of Bingen: A Visionary Life*, 2nd ed. (London: Routledge, 1998), 100.

20. Barbara Newman, "'Sybil of the Rhine': Hildegard's Life and Times," in Newman, *Voice of the Living Light*, 1.

21. Meconi, "Hildegard's *Lingua ignota*," 75.

22. Ibid., 70–76.

23. Hildegard of Bingen, *The Book of the Rewards of Life (Liber Vitae Meritorum)*, trans. Bruce W. Hozeski (New York: Oxford University Press, 1994), 281.

24. Hildegard of Bingen, *Explanation of the Rule of Benedict*, trans. Hugh Feiss (Toronto: Peregrina Publishing, 1998), 23.

25. Hildegard of Bingen, *Homilies on the Gospels*, trans. Beverly Mayne Kienzle, Cistercian Study Series 241 (Collegeville, MN: Liturgical Press, 2011), 6–7.

26. Giles Constable, "Hildegard's Explanation of the Rule of St Benedict," in Haverkamp, *Hildegard von Bingen in ihrem historischen Umfeld*, 166.

27. Constant J. Mews, "Hildegard of Bingen and the Hirsau Reform in Germany 1080–1180," in *A Companion to Hildegard of Bingen*, ed. Beverly Mayne Kienzle, Debra L. Stoudt, and George Ferzoco, Brill's Companions to the Christian Tradition 45 (Leiden: Brill, 2014), 80.

28. Anna Silvas, *Jutta and Hildegard: The Biographical Sources*, Medieval Women: Texts and Contexts 1 (Turnhout, Belgium: Brepols, 1998), 160.

29. *The Letters of Hildegard of Bingen*, 3 vols., trans. Joseph L. Baird and Radd K. Ehrman (New York: Oxford University Press, 1994–2004), 1:78.

30. The following comparison of the two manuscripts is based on Barbara Newman's detailed discussion in Saint Hildegard of Bingen, *Symphonia: A Critical Edition of the Symphonia armonie celestium revelationum* [Symphony of the Harmony of Celestial Revelations], 2nd ed., introduction, translations, and commentary by Barbara Newman (Ithaca, NY: Cornell University Press, 1998), 51–60.

31. Book 3, vision 6.

32. Newman, *Symphonia*, 57.

33. Table based on ibid., 55–56.

34. Virginia Woolf, *A Room of One's Own* (London: Harcourt, Brace, and World, 1929).

Chapter 5. Expansion

1. Beverly Mayne Kienzle, *Hildegard and Her Gospel Homilies: Speaking New Mysteries*, Medieval Women: Texts and Contexts 12 (Turnhout, Belgium: Brepols, 2009), xii.

2. Anna Silvas, *Jutta and Hildegard: The Biographical Sources*, Medieval Women: Texts and Contexts 1 (Turnhout, Belgium: Brepols, 1998), 191.

3. Kienzle, *Hildegard of Bingen and Her Gospel Homilies*, 47–57.

4. Silvas, *Jutta and Hildegard*, 25.

5. Ibid., 26 and 131, but see Constant J. Mews, "Hildegard and the Schools," in *Hildegard of Bingen: The Context of Her Thought and Art*, ed. Charles Burnett and Peter Dronke (London: Warburg Institute, 1998),100.

6. Kienzle, *Hildegard of Bingen and Her Gospel Homilies*, 76–78.

7. The language here is taken from the evocative translation of Christopher Page in Abbess Hildegard of Bingen, *Sequences and Hymns*, ed. Christopher Page, Medieval Church Music 1 (Moretonhampstead, Newton Abbot: Antico Edition, 1983), 19.

8. Felix Heinzer outlines the stark differences between standard Eucharius fare and Hildegard's *O Euchari columba*; see Heinzer, "Unequal Twins: Visionary Attitude and Monastic Culture in Elisabeth of Schönau and Hildegard of Bingen," in *A Companion to Hildegard of Bingen*, ed. Beverly Mayne Kienzle, Debra L. Stoudt, and George Ferzoco, Brill's Companions to the Christian Tradition 45 (Leiden: Brill, 2014), 98.

9. Silvas, *Jutta and Hildegard*, 246–48.

10. Barbara Newman, "'Sybil of the Rhine': Hildegard's Life and Times," in *Voice of the Living Light: Hildegard of Bingen and Her World*, ed. Barbara Newman (Berkeley: University of California Press, 1998), 18.

11. Silvas, *Jutta and Hildegard*, 267–68.

12. It was thought that the new house arose on the remnants of a deserted Augustinian double foundation created in 1148 but later destroyed by imperial troops; see Werner Lauter, "The Old Convent of Eibingen," in *Hildegard of Bingen: Historical Sites*, 2nd English ed., Hagiography and Iconography 40121 (Regensburg, Germany: Schnell & Steiner, 2008), 19. For the revised view of Hildegard's connection to Eibingen, see Matthias Schmandt, "Hildegard von Bingen und das Kloster Eibingen: Revision einer historischen Überlieferung," *Nassauische Annalen: Jahrbuch des Vereins für Nassauische Altertumskunde und Geschichtsforschung* 125 (2014): 29–52.

13. Silvas, *Jutta and Hildegard*, 268.

14. The introduction may or may not be intended for the vita; see Hildegard of Bingen, *Two Hagiographies: Vita sancti Rupperti confessoris, Vita sancti Dysibodi episcopi*, trans. Hugh Feiss, ed. Christopher P. Evans, Dallas Medieval Texts and Translations 11 (Paris: Peeters, 2010), 5.

15. Ibid., 45.

16. Newman, *Symphonia*, 295 (with the wrong year of dedication).

17. Hildegard of Bingen, *An Explanation of the Athanasian Creed*, trans. Thomas M. Izbicki (Toronto: Peregrina, 2001), 9.

18. *The Letters of Hildegard of Bingen*, 3 vols., trans. Joseph L. Baird and Radd K. Ehrman (New York: Oxford University Press, 1994–2004), 1:149–50.

19. Silvas, *Jutta and Hildegard*, 205.

20. Ibid., 206.

Chapter 6. After Volmar

1. *The Letters of Hildegard of Bingen*, 3 vols., trans. Joseph L. Baird and Radd K. Ehrman (New York: Oxford University Press, 1994–2004), 2:196.

2. Anna Silvas, *Jutta and Hildegard: The Biographical Sources*, Medieval Women: Texts and Contexts 1 (Turnhout, Belgium: Brepols, 1998), 155–56.

3. Madeline Caviness, "Artist: To See, Hear, and Know All at Once," in *Voice of the Living Light: Hildegard of Bingen and Her World*, ed. Barbara Newman (Berkeley: University of California Press, 1998), 121–22.

4. Madeline H. Caviness, "Hildegard as Designer of the Illustrations to Her Works," in *Hildegard of Bingen: The Context of Her Thought and Art*, ed. Charles Burnett and Peter Dronke (London: Warburg Institute, 1998), 34–41.

5. Silvas, *Jutta and Hildegard*, 179.

6. Barbara Newman, "Three-Part Invention: The *Vita S. Hildegardis* and Mystical Hagiography," in Burnett and Dronke, *Hildegard of Bingen*, 196–97.

7. Barbara Newman, "Hildegard and Her Hagiographers: The Remaking of Female Sainthood," in *Gendered Voices: Medieval Saints and Their Interpreters*, ed. Catherine M. Mooney (Philadelphia: University of Pennsylvania Press, 1999).

8. Silvas, *Jutta and Hildegard*, 123–24.

9. Newman, "Hildegard and Her Hagiographers," 32–33.

10. Silvas, *Jutta and Hildegard*, 220–37.

11. *Letters of Hildegard of Bingen*, 2:30.

12. Joan Ferrante, "Correspondent: 'Blessed Is the Speech of Your Mouth,'" in *Voice of the Living Light: Hildegard of Bingen and Her World*, ed. Barbara Newman (Berkeley: University of California Press, 1998), 99.

13. Hildegard of Bingen, *Solutions to Thirty-Eight Questions*, trans. Beverly Mayne Kienzle with Jenny C. Bledsoe and Stephen H. Behnke, Cistercian Study Series 253 (Collegeville, MN: Liturgical Press, 2014), 1.

14. Ibid., 66 and 76.

15. *Letters of Hildegard of Bingen*, 2:18.

16. Ibid., 2:20.

17. Ibid., 2:23–24.

18. Caviness, "Artist," 114.

19. Laurence Moulinier, "Unterhaltungen mit dem Teufel: Eine französische Hildegardvita des 15. Jahrhunderts und ihre Quellen," in *Hildegard von Bingen in ihrem historischen Umfeld: Internationaler wissenschaftlicher Kongreß zum 900jährigen Jubiläum, 13.–19. September 1998, Bingen am Rhein*, ed. Alfred Haverkamp (Mainz, Germany: Verlag Philipp von Zabern, 2000), 519–60.

20. Mary Berry and Franklyn Gellnick, "Cistercian Monks" in *The New Grove Dictionary of Music and Musicians*, 2nd ed. (New York: Macmillan, 2001).

21. Newman, "Hildegard and Her Hagiographers," 198.

22. Text given in Johann Baptiste Pitra, *Analecta Sanctae Hildegardis*, Analecta sacra 8 (Montecassino, Italy, 1882; reprt. ed., Farnsborough, UK: Gregg, 1966), 439–40. No music is known to survive.

23. Silvas, *Jutta and Hildegard*, 99–117.

24. Ibid., 101.

25. It was appended to his letter to Bovo.

26. *Letters of Hildegard of Bingen*, 1:81.

27. Ibid., 1:77.

28. Ibid., 1:77–78.

29. Ibid., 1:78.

30. Ibid.

31. Ibid., 1:79.

32. Ibid.

33. Ibid.

34. Silvas, *Jutta and Hildegard*, 260.

35. Ibid., 209.

Chapter 7. Aftermath

1. Anna Silvas, *Jutta and Hildegard: The Biographical Sources*, Medieval Women: Texts and Contexts 1 (Turnhout, Belgium: Brepols, 1998), 216 (my translation).

2. Barbara Newman, "Hildegard and Her Hagiographers: The Remaking of Female Sainthood," in *Gendered Voices: Medieval Saints and Their Interpreters*, ed. Catherine M. Mooney (Philadelphia: University of Pennsylvania Press, 1999), 30.

3. On the reception of Hildegard's writings, see Michael Embach, "Hildegard of Bingen (1098–1179): A History of Reception," in *A Companion to Hildegard of Bingen*, ed. Beverly Mayne Kienzle, Debra L. Stoudt, and George Ferzoco, Brill's Companions to the Christian Tradition 45 (Leiden: Brill, 2014), 273–304.

4. Silvas, *Jutta and Hildegard*, 258.

5. Ibid., 270; see also 268.

6. George Ferzoco, "The Canonization and Doctorization of Hildegard of Bingen," in Kienzle, Stoudt, and Ferzoco, *Companion to Hildegard of Bingen*, 306.

7. Silvas, *Jutta and Hildegard*, 269.

8. Ferzoco, "Canonization and Doctorization," 308.

9. Madeline H. Caviness, "Hildegard as Designer of the Illustrations to Her Works," in *Hildegard of Bingen: The Context of Her Thought and Art*, ed. Charles Burnett and Peter Dronke (London: Warburg Institute, 1998), 29.

10. The state secularized the monastery in 1803, but the nuns did not leave until 1814. See Jennifer Bain, *Hildegard of Bingen and Musical Reception: The Modern Revival of a Medieval Composer* (Cambridge, UK: Cambridge University Press, 2015), 74.

11. Johann Konrad Dahl, *Die heilige Hildegard, Äbtissin in dem Kloster Rupertsberg bei Bingen: Eine historische Abhandlung* (Mainz, Germany: Florian Kupferberg, 1832).

12. See the detailed description in Honey Meconi, "The Unknown Hildegard: Editing, Performance, and Reception (An *Ordo Virtutum* in Five Acts)," in *Music in Print and Beyond:*

Hildegard von Bingen to The Beatles, ed. Craig A. Monson and Roberta Montemorra Marvin (Rochester, NY: University of Rochester Press, 2013), 258–305.

13. Hildegard von Bingen, *Lieder*, ed. Pudentiana Barth, M. Immaculata Ritscher, and Joseph Schmidt-Görg (Salzburg, Germany: Otto Müller Verlag, 1969).

14. Hildegard von Bingen, *Symphonia armonie celestium revelationum*, 8 vols., ed. Marianne Richert Pfau (Bryn Mawr, PA: Hildegard Publishing, 1997–1998).

15. See Bain, *Hildegard of Bingen*, 70–100, on Schneider's role in the general Hildegard revival.

16. Christopher Page, personal communication (e-mail), July 24, 2016.

17. Abbess Hildegard of Bingen, *Sequences and Hymns*, ed. Christopher Page, Medieval Church Music 1 (Moretonhampstead, Newton Abbot: Antico Edition, 1983).

18. Jennifer Bain, "Hildegard on 34th Street: Chant in the Marketplace," *Echo: A Music-Centered Journal* 6, no. 1 (2004). The first recording is from 1948; see Bain, *Hildegard of Bingen*, 30.

Chapter 8. Hildegard's Music: An Overview

1. Hildegard of Bingen, *Scivias*, trans. Mother Columba Hart and Jane Bishop, intro. Barbara J. Newman, preface Caroline Walker Bynum (New York: Paulist Press, 1990), 163.

2. Florence Eliza Glaze, "Medical Writer: 'Behold the Human Creature,'" in *Voice of the Living Light: Hildegard of Bingen and Her World*, ed. Barbara Newman (Berkeley: University of California Press, 1998), 239.

3. Saint Hildegard of Bingen, *Symphonia: A Critical Edition of the Symphonia armonie celestium revelationum [Symphony of the Harmony of Celestial Revelations]*, 2nd ed., introduction, translations, and commentary by Barbara Newman (Ithaca, NY: Cornell University Press, 1998), 289.

4. *The Letters of Hildegard of Bingen*, 3 vols., trans. Joseph L. Baird and Radd K. Ehrman (New York: Oxford University Press, 1994–2004), 1:14–15.

5. Hildegard, *Scivias*, 344, 351.

6. Hildegard of Bingen, *The Book of the Rewards of Life (Liber Vitae Meritorum)*, trans. Bruce W. Hozeski (New York: Oxford University Press, 1994), 39.

7. *Letters of Hildegard of Bingen*, 1:57.

8. Ibid., 2:199.

9. Hildegard, *Book of the Rewards of Life*, 10.

10. Hildegard, *Scivias*, 195.

11. *Letters of Hildegard of Bingen*, 2:181.

12. Hildegard, *Book of the Rewards of Life*, 187.

13. Hildegard, *Scivias*, 139ff.

14. Hildegard, *Book of the Rewards of Life*, 211.

15. *Letters of Hildegard of Bingen*, 3:194.

16. Hildegard, *Scivias*, 210.

17. Hildegard, *Book of the Rewards of Life*, 205.

18. Ibid., 202.

19. *Letters of Hildegard of Bingen*, 1:79.

20. Ibid., 3:194.

21. Ibid., 3:184.

22. Hildegard, *Scivias*, 206.

23. Beverly Mayne Kienzle, *Hildegard and Her Gospel Homilies: Speaking New Mysteries*, Medieval Women: Texts and Contexts 12 (Turnhout, Belgium: Brepols, 2009), 58, quoting the *Liber divinorum operum*.

24. Hildegard, *Book of the Rewards of Life*, 275.

25. Ibid., 276.

26. Ibid., 278.

27. Ibid., 275–81.

28. Hildegard, *Symphonia*, 68–73.

29. Marianne Richert Pfau and Stefan J. Morent, *Hildegard von Bingen: Der Klang des Himmels*, Europäische Komponistinnen 1 (Cologne: Böhlau Verlag, 2005), 182–83; Barbara Stühlmeyer, *Die Gesänge der Hildegard von Bingen: Eine musikologische, theologische und kulturhistorische Untersuchung*, Studien und Materialien zur Musikwissenschaft 30 (Hildesheim, Germany: Georg Olms Verlag, 2003), 191–291.

30. For example, see Pfau and Morent, *Hildegard von Bingen*, 202–213.

31. The Germanic-sounding "heu heu" in *O dulcissime amator* is a Latin expression of pain or dismay. In addition to *O ecclesia*, *Ordo virtutum* contains some German as well.

32. Hildegard, *Symphonia*, 45.

33. Ibid., 40.

34. Joan Cadden, "It Takes All Kinds: Sexuality and Gender Difference in Hildegard of Bingen's 'Book of Compound Medicine,'" *Traditio* 40 (1984): 157.

35. On the Jesse tree, see Margot Fassler, "Composer and Dramatist: 'Melodious Singing and the Freshness of Remorse,'" in Newman, *Voice of the Living Light*, 156ff.

36. Hildegard, *Symphonia*, 280.

37. Fassler, "Composer and Dramatist," 167; *eadem*, "Allegorical Architecture in *Scivias*: Hildegard's Setting for the *Ordo Virtutum*," *Journal of the American Musicological Society* 67 (2014): 360–61; and "*Vox Feminae*: Barbara Thornton on Hildegard of Bingen," in Bernard D. Sherman, *Inside Early Music: Conversations with Performers* (New York: Oxford University Press, 1997), 64.

38. Jürg Stenzl, "Wie hat 'Hildegard vom Disibodenberg und Rupertsberg' komponiert? Ein analytischer Versuch mit den E-Antiphonen und dem *Ordo Virtutum*," *Archiv für Musikwissenschaft* 64 (2007): 199.

39. Jennifer Bain, "Hooked on Ecstasy: Performance 'Practice' and the Reception of the Music of Hildegard of Bingen," in *The Sounds and Sights of Performance in Early Music: Essays in Honour of Timothy J. McGee*, ed. Maureen Epp and Brian E. Powell (Farnham, Surrey: Ashgate, 2009), 253–73, and *eadem*, "Hildegard, Hermannus, and Late Chant Style," *Journal of Music Theory* 52 (2008): 123–49.

40. Pfau and Morent, *Hildegard von Bingen*, 185–201.

41. David Hiley, *Western Plainchant: A Handbook* (Oxford: Clarendon Press, 1993), 138.

42. Rebecca Maloy, "*Scolica Enchiriadis* and the 'Non-Diatonic' Plainsong Tradition," *Early Music History* 28 (2009): 76.

43. Willi Apel, *Gregorian Chant* (Bloomington: Indiana University Press, 1958), 248.

44. Pfau and Morent, *Hildegard von Bingen*, 285–310; Bain, "Hooked on Ecstasy;" *eadem*, "Hildegard, Hermannus, and Late Chant Style."

45. Tova Leigh-Choate, William T. Flynn, and Margot E. Fassler, "Hearing the Heavenly Symphony: An Overview of Hildegard's Musical Oeuvre with Case Studies," in *A Companion to Hildegard of Bingen*, ed. Beverly Mayne Kienzle, Debra L. Stoudt, and George Ferzoco, Brill's Companions to the Christian Tradition 45 (Leiden: Brill, 2014), 181–82.

Chapter 9. Liturgy and Shorter Genres

1. *The Letters of Hildegard of Bingen*, 3 vols., trans. Joseph L. Baird and Radd K. Ehrman (New York: Oxford University Press, 1994–2004), 3:97 (Letter 296r); 1:76–77 (Letter 23, to the prelates of Mainz).

2. Anna Silvas, *Jutta and Hildegard: The Biographical Sources*, Medieval Women: Texts and Contexts 1 (Turnhout, Belgium: Brepols, 1998), 25.

3. Margot Fassler, "Composer and Dramatist: 'Melodious Singing and the Freshness of Remorse,'" in *Voice of the Living Light: Hildegard of Bingen and Her World*, ed. Barbara Newman (Berkeley: University of California Press, 1998), 160.

4. Tova Leigh-Choate, William T. Flynn, and Margot E. Fassler, "Hearing the Heavenly Symphony: An Overview of Hildegard's Musical Oeuvre with Case Studies," in *A Companion to Hildegard of Bingen*, ed. Beverly Mayne Kienzle, Debra L. Stoudt, and George Ferzoco, Brill's Companions to the Christian Tradition 45 (Leiden: Brill, 2014), 174.

5. Marianne Richert Pfau and Stefan J. Morent, *Hildegard von Bingen: Der Klang des Himmels*, Europäische Komponistinnen 1 (Cologne: Böhlau Verlag, 2005), 253–54.

6. Kyrie 97, as seen in David Hiley, *Western Plainchant: A Handbook* (Oxford: Clarendon Press, 1993), 156. Lara Housez was the first to notice the connection.

7. Barbara Stühlmeyer, *Die Gesänge der Hildegard von Bingen: Eine musikologische, theologische und kulturhistorische Untersuchung*, Studien und Materialien zur Musikwissenschaft 30 (Hildesheim, Germany: Georg Olms Verlag, 2003), 71–72.

8. Fassler, "Composer and Dramatist," 154.

9. Ibid.

10. Pfau and Morent, *Hildegard von Bingen*, 74.

Chapter 10. Longer Genres

1. Marianne Richert Pfau and Stefan J. Morent, *Hildegard von Bingen: Der Klang des Himmels*, Europäische Komponistinnen 1 (Cologne: Böhlau Verlag, 2005), 67.

2. John Stevens, "The Musical Individuality of Hildegard's Songs: A Liturgical Shadowland," in *Hildegard of Bingen: The Context of Her Thought and Art*, ed. Charles Burnett and Peter Dronke (London: Warburg Institute, 1998), 185–87.

3. Barbara Stühlmeyer, *Die Gesänge der Hildegard von Bingen: Eine musikologische, theologische und kulturhistorische Untersuchung*, Studien und Materialien zur Musikwissenschaft 30 (Hildesheim, Germany: Georg Olms Verlag, 2003), 120–21,

4. Anna Silvas, *Jutta and Hildegard: The Biographical Sources*, Medieval Women: Texts and Contexts 1 (Turnhout, Belgium: Brepols, 1998), 263.

5. Saint Hildegard of Bingen, *Symphonia: A Critical Edition of the Symphonia armonie celestium revelationum [Symphony of the Harmony of Celestial Revelations]*, 2nd ed., introduc-

tion, translations, and commentary by Barbara Newman (Ithaca, NY: Cornell University Press, 1998), 73.

6. The most recent interpretation is Margot Fassler, "Music for the Love Feast: Hildegard of Bingen and the Song of Songs," in *Resonant Witness: Conversations between Music and Theology*, ed. Jeremy S. Begbie and Steven R. Guthrie (Grand Rapids, MI: William B. Eerdmans, 2011), 367–73.

7. Peter Dronke, "The Composition of Hildegard of Bingen's *Symphonia*," *Sacris erudiri: Jahrboek voor Godsdienstwetenschappen* 19 (1969–1970): 389.

List of Works

Information on critical editions and English translations may be found in Honey Meconi, "Hildegard of Bingen," in *Oxford Bibliographies in Music*, ed. Bruce Gustafson (New York: Oxford University Press, 2017).

1. Flats appear inconsistently both within a composition and across different manuscripts.

2. *Mathias sanctus* is identified as a hymn in its sole source but follows the form of a sequence. Brackets mean that genre indication is missing in the manuscript[s].

3. *O cruor sanguinis* is missing the final phrase in its sole source, but musically a D final is expected.

4. *O dulcissime amator* has many problems of transmission. The Dendermonde reading has numerous B-flats, but only in sections that appear to have been erroneously transposed.

5. *O quam preciosa* uses both B-flat and E-flat.

6. *Unde quocumque* has serious transmission problems; the intended final is unclear.

SELECTED BIBLIOGRAPHY

Flanagan, Sabina. *Hildegard of Bingen, 1098–1179: A Visionary Life*. 2nd ed. London: Routledge, 1998. A book-length introduction to Hildegard's life and works, including a chapter on music that emphasizes her texts.

Hildegard of Bingen. *The Letters of Hildegard of Bingen*. 3 vols. Translated by Joseph L. Baird and Radd K. Ehrman. New York: Oxford University Press, 1994–2004. English translations of Hildegard's correspondence, comprising almost 400 letters and their responses.

——. *Lieder: Faksimile Riesencodex (Hs. 2) der Hessischen Landesbibliothek Wiesbaden fol. 466–481v*. Edited by Lorenz Welker. Commentary by Michael Klaper. Elementa musicae 1. Wiesbaden, Germany: Dr. Ludwig Reichert Verlag, 1998. The music section of the main manuscript of Hildegard's works, presented in full-size color facsimile with a detailed English-language commentary.

——. *Symphonia: A Critical Edition of the Symphonia armonie celestium revelationum (Symphony of the Harmony of the Celestial Revelations)*. 2nd ed. Introduction, translations, and commentary by Barbara Newman. Ithaca, NY: Cornell University Press, 1998. A critical edition of Hildegard's song texts, with both poetic and literal English translations, extensive background material, and commentary. Marianne Richert Pfau provides a short musical discussion.

Kienzle, Beverly Mayne, Debra L. Stoudt, and George Ferzoco, eds. *A Companion to Hildegard of Bingen*. Brill's Companions to the Christian Tradition 45. Leiden: Brill, 2014. Fourteen essays discussing varied aspects of Hildegard's life, work, and reception, with two essays on her music.

Kotzur, Hans-Jürgen, ed. *Hildegard von Bingen 1098–1179*. Mainz, Germany: Verlag Philipp von Zabern, 1998. This iconography of Hildegard contains more than 250 illustrations, most in color, documenting manifold aspects of her life and reception up to 1998.

Meconi, Honey. "Hildegard of Bingen." In *Oxford Bibliographies in Music*. Edited by Bruce Gustafson. New York: Oxford University Press, 2017. Annotated bibliography of 150 important publications about Hildegard's life, music, other creations, and reception.

Newman, Barbara. *Sister of Wisdom: St. Hildegard's Theology of the Feminine*. 2nd ed. Berkeley: University of California Press, 1997. A highly readable explanation of Hildegard's theology from a feminist perspective, with many references to the texts of her music.

Newman, Barbara, ed. *Voice of the Living Light: Hildegard of Bingen and Her World*. Berkeley: University of California Press, 1998. Multiple authors tackle different aspects of Hildegard's life and work in this excellent collection that includes separate essays on her music and poetry.

Pfau, Marianne Richert, and Stefan Morent. *Hildegard von Bingen: Der Klang des Himmels*. Europäische Komponistinnen 1. Cologne: Böhlau Verlag, 2005. This book on Hildegard's music is especially strong in musical analysis and explanation of Hildegard's sometimes idiosyncratic notation.

Silvas, Anna. *Jutta and Hildegard: The Biographical Sources*. Medieval Women: Texts and Contexts 1. Turnhout, Belgium: Brepols, 1998. English translations and discussion of the most important sources for Hildegard's biography, including her vita, Jutta's vita, and the thirteenth-century brief for Hildegard's canonization.

Stühlmeyer, Barbara. *Die Gesänge der Hildegard von Bingen: Eine musikologische, theologische und kulturhistorische Untersuchung*. Studien und Materialien zur Musikwissenschaft 30. Hildesheim, Germany: Georg Olms Verlag, 2003. A thorough introduction to Hildegard's music that places her compositions in the context of both other chant of her time and medieval music theory. Additional features include an extensive discography.

SELECTED DISCOGRAPHY

All of Hildegard's compositions have been recorded, some many times. Precisely how to perform twelfth-century plainchant is unknown; the following items demonstrate various approaches to the music. The first three items are foundational recordings of Hildegard's music and provide a ready introduction to her output. The next seven display a range of performing interpretations based on straightforward readings of the music. The final three use Hildegard's compositions as a starting point for highly creative reimaginings of the compositions.

A Feather on the Breath of God: Sequences and Hymns by Abbess Hildegard of Bingen (Gothic Voices, directed by Christopher Page) Hyperion CDA66039. The recording that did more than any other to launch the popularity of Hildegard's music, with famed early music singer Emma Kirkby and others performing a selection of hymns and sequences.

900 Years: Hildegard von Bingen. (Sequentia) BMG/Deutsche harmonia mundi 0 5472 77505 2. A boxed set of eight CDs, containing most of Hildegard's music, by a leading medieval ensemble that played an important role in reviving her music. CDs also available individually.

The Complete Hildegard von Bingen, Vols. 1–3 (Sinfonye, directed by Stevie Wishart) Celestial Harmonies 13127-2, 13128-2, and 13129-2. The first three entries, available separately, in a projected "Complete Works" cycle by an ensemble noted for their exploration of medieval women's music: (1) *Symphony of the Harmony of Celestial Revelations*; (2) *Aurora*; (3) *O nobilissima viriditas.*

Symphonia harmoniae caelestium revelationum (Schola der Benediktinerinnenabtei St. Hildegard Rüdesheim-Eibingen) Bayer Records 100 116. One of several recordings made by the nuns of Hildegard's reconstituted abbey, with selections from the Symphonia, *Ordo virtutum,* and the modern First Vespers for Hildegard.

11,000 Virgins: Chants for the Feast of St. Ursula (Anonymous 4) Harmonia mundi HMU 907200. On this first of their two Hildegard CDs, the renowned female quartet sings a partial reconstruction of three Offices for St. Ursula using Hildegard's compositions and anonymous plainchant.

Laudes de Sainte Ursule (Ensemble Organum, directed by Marcel Pérès) Harmonia mundi HMC 901626. A reconstruction of Lauds for St. Ursula (different from that by Anonymous 4), performed in Ensemble Organum's distinctive folk-influenced, ornamental style.

Ordo virtutum (Sequentia) BMG/Deutsche harmonia mundi 77051-2-RG. The first recording of Hildegard's play with music, in an imaginative and powerful rendition that is significantly different from Sequentia's later version in their boxed set.

O nobilissima viriditas (Catherine Schroeder) Champeaux CSM 0006. An elegant compilation with spare performances by a soloist joined at times by one more voice, with minimal accompaniment.

Voices of Angels: Music of Hildegard von Bingen (Voices of Ascension, directed by Dennis Keene) Delos DE 3219. Fine singing, both solo and choral, on this unaccompanied all-woman recording.

Celestial Harmonies: Responsories and Antiphons from Symphoniae armonie celestium revelationum (Oxford Camerata, directed by Jeremy Summerly) Naxos 8.557983. The second of two recordings by this group, one of the few to perform Hildegard's music by male as well as female singers in acknowledgment of the possession of her music by the male Cistercian monastery of Villers. Attractive unaccompanied singing in a straightforward performance.

Ursula 11: Hildegard von Bingen (Psallentes, directed by Hendrik Vanden Abeele) Le Bricoleur LBCD/03. Beautiful singing by a choir of female voices in inventive renditions of nine Ursula songs.

Music from Symphonia harmonia celestium revelationum (Alba) Classico CLASSCD 198. One of the most creative interpretations of Hildegard's songs, with a strong instrumental presence.

Vision: The Music of Hildegard von Bingen (Richard Souther) Angel CDC 7243 5 55246 2 1. The best known of the many New Age–inspired recordings.

INDEX

HONEY MECONI is Chair and Professor of Music in the College Music Department and Professor of Musicology at the Eastman School of Music at the University of Rochester. Her many books include *Pierre de la Rue and Musical Life at the Habsburg-Burgundian Court*. She is a co-winner of the Noah Greenberg Award for "distinguished contribution to the study and performance of early music."

WOMEN

Composers

Kaija Saariaho
  Pirkko Moisala

Marga Richter
  Sharon Mirchandani

Hildegard of Bingen
  Honey Meconi

The University of Illinois Press

is a founding member of the

Association of American University Presses.

———————————————————————

University of Illinois Press

1325 South Oak Street

Champaign, IL 61820-6903

www.press.uillinois.edu

Made in the USA
Thornton, CO
01/07/25 14:41:28

dd836d67-aecf-405f-8c70-0384654e4916R02